Within Tweeting Distance

How States Use Twitter Diplomacy

Noor Suwwan

Within Tweeting Distance
How States Use Twitter Diplomacy

Noor Suwwan

Academica Press
Washington~London

Library of Congress Cataloging-in-Publication Data

Names: Suwwan, Noor (author)
Title: Within tweeting distance : how states use twitter diplomacy | Suwwan, Noor.
Description: Washington : Academica Press, 2022. | Includes references.
Identifiers: LCCN 2021952080 | ISBN 9781680532838 (hardcover) | 9781680532845 (e-book)

Acknowledgements

To Dr. Imene Ajala- my advisor- the most knowledgeable person I know and the most hardworking person I have met: you've influenced me in ways you and I both don't fully realize. To the department of IR at the University of Wollongong in Dubai: what you've created is a graduate program par excellence in the heart of the Middle East with a voluntary attendance rate that constantly amazes me.

To all those who came before me: thank you for the volumes of knowledge you have produced. To all those who will come after me: thank you for the volumes of knowledge you will produce. To scholars of IR of the Middle East, present and past: the extent of the influence of your words will never truly be captured by citation-counts; they reach far beyond the limits you've allowed yourself to imagine thanks to rigid academic standards of recognition.

Contents

Foreword

It all started with the Arab Spring. I was 16 at the time. Too unconscious of my own ignorance of the realities in the Arab world. Too unconscious of the extent of my knowledge on the inverse of realities in the Arab world. That inverse of realities I now call the Arab cyberspace. At 16, I thought I made a discovery that I genuinely thought no one else had noticed; blogs! Blogs that were written by people who wrote from an Arabic perspective on social issues, events on the ground and politics. There were countless blogs of a literary nature; poems, essays, stories, entire novels with chapters released one blogpost at a time.

At that time, I got into the habit of collecting commercial books and media works about the Middle East. A task I didn't seem to be doing a very good job at, given my location. The 'Middle East' section at 3 local bookstores only displayed Jean Sasson and Khaled Housseini. Similarly, I was attempting to collect media works on the Arab world from Arabic media. Arabic media has a rich history and an even richer present. Yet, it was clear to me even during my teens that there seemed to be what looked like a schism. A schism between mainstream narratives and the monotonous implied narratives within most Arabic media works. What this created is an entire generation that grew up feeling simply 'different,' because every

Arabic millennial kid thought he was the only one having those particular experiences, a natural byproduct of the lack of representation on state TV channels, radios, news, TV shows and even mainstream songs. So naturally, my accidental discovery had a strong pull for me. It offered an avenue for *some* representation. I read and read for hours on my dial-up internet connection countless blogs that represented authentic Arab voices. Some were blogging about the war in Lebanon, some on harassment on the streets of Amman, some of what it means to be a Muslim feminist. There were serious inquiries on the blogosphere on what it means to be Arabic, what it means to be a Muslim and what it means to reconcile the two. There were well-educated young writers who were debating with themselves (publicly) how to reconcile the old and new, tradition and modernity in today's Middle East. All in broken English. And broken Arabic. And somehow the authenticity of the writings, the capability of their pens and the critical examination of the expired solutions of yesterday produced an experiment in literary beauty. And norm entrepreneurship. I always wondered if these blogs were supposed to be private online journals, which were accidentally made public through a technical glitch. Sometimes, I wondered if I should 'comment' on one of the blog posts that I found particularly daring with a *'dude, do you know people can actually read these entries?'*

Shocked as I was, the gravitational field of the blogosphere was so strong that I continued to read on almost religiously. And it seems I wasn't alone in reading them, remembering them or being largely influenced by them. Soon social media platforms came along, expediting some of the active users and readers of the blogosphere to the Twittersphere and the general cybersphere. In this book, I make the argument that it was this blogosphere that sparked the change process in traditional Arab societies.

10 years later, I still read. While yesterday's blogpost, blogger and WordPress had transformed into today's most important platform: Twitter. But this time, my internet was better, my device smaller, my political fluency higher and my lens a lot more academic. And this time, I wasn't one of barely 25 people who realized that something novel is unfolding, the entire world seemed to be in the know of the potency of the Twittersphere (as I will outline in more detail in the book). The parallels I see between my first scrolling experience and my second one of the blogosphere and Twittersphere, respectively are extraordinary. The most important of which is the stubborn ignoring of both.

While exploring the Twittersphere, I kept a close eye on the emerging literature on Twitter Diplomacy. The lack of theoretical frameworks within this new sub-field of IR became very apparent. This pushed me to want to propose a theoretical framework, based on the patterns that I had already begun to observe in the hopes of contributing to the literature of Twitter Diplomacy. The theoretical framework was then tested on Arab state-actors specifically, which also fills a margin of space not very well inhabited within the literature.

The book, like a lot of academic books, began as my graduate dissertation. And was expanded and reformatted into a book that aims to be accessible to the general-interest reader. Even though, the original conformity to the strict confines of academic writing has been reformatted to a more accessible form of writing, it is still an academic book that attempts to maintain the highest standards of academic rigor. Hence, to appease this dual purpose of the book, one of the steps that has been undertaken is to include a visual presentation of some of the Tweets in the form of screenshots. Another step is to refrain from in-text references and include the references as end-notes.

Introduction

In the leaked voice record between Prince Hamzah Bin Hussein and the man who identified himself as the head of the army after the alleged coup attempt in Jordan, the man explicitly asks Prince Hamzah to 'cease his tweeting activities' (1). A perfectly timed demand that strengthens the argument within this book; that the tweeting patterns of Arab state-actors are an academically unexplored area and demand urgent attention because of their serious implications. Indeed, mid-coup-allegations Prince Hamzah's mother Queen Noor tweeted:

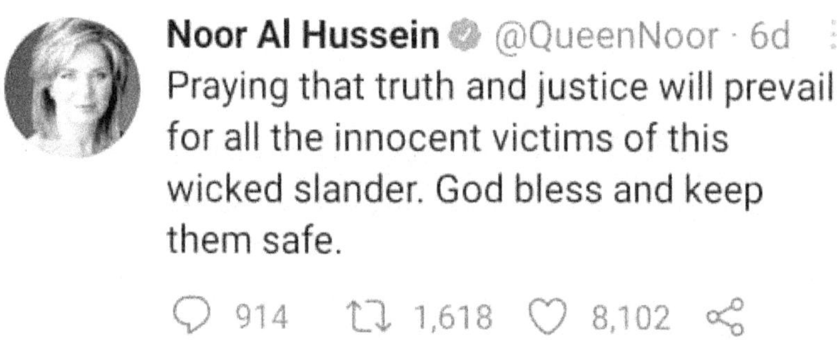

Tweet 1 – Queen Noor's Tweet

While Prince Hamzah still did not address the public after the leaked record, Queen Noor continued to tweet:

Tweet 2- Queen Noor's 2nd Tweet

In fact, to have one of the major demands to an actor who is perceived to be compromising the stability of the state be 'stop tweeting' is a testimony to the actual or perceived potency of Twittersphere in shaping political discourse within states. Or maybe just Arab states. Especially after the mistake that academics (and state-actors) committed in neglecting investigating the ignored Arab blogosphere and its links to the Arab Spring, academics should not commit this mistake again by neglecting the Arab Twittersphere. Which I argue in this book is the rightful heir to the Arab blogosphere.

This study attempts to answer a question that may seem obvious at the beginning: who is Arab state-actors tweeting for? Or in other words, who are they speaking to? In attempting to answer this question and after extensive familiarization with the Twitter Diplomacy literature and the Arab Twittersphere, a classification framework has been developed that is thought to be useful in identifying who the ‘main’ audience of a Tweet is. And hence this is a study of both the audience of Arab state-actors Tweets’ and the utility of the developed classification framework. In doing so the study identifies interesting trends in the Arab Twittersphere and generates a few unexpected results.

Part I:
Exploring

Chapter 1:
Diplomacy – a brief overview

Introduction

In presenting the story of Twitter Diplomacy, I have to present a few sub-stories that will serve as background knowledge to a few concepts from overlapping subfields of IR. They are intended to serve as pillars to understanding the proposed arguments within this book. The first chapter will be the story of Diplomacy. It is not within the scope of this chapter to provide an exhaustive, analytical or reflexive review of diplomacy. And hence this chapter has been kept brief and traditional. The purpose of this chapter is to narrate that new actors have emerged as legitimate diplomatic actors and that Twitter Diplomacy has emerged as the time-and-place-specific diplomatic practice of our time.

Chapter objectives:

1.1 All the Definitions:
- A traditional definition of Diplomacy
- The difference between Diplomacy and Foreign Policy
- What is Public Diplomacy

1.2 Why Twitter Diplomacy necessitates a Constructivist lens of IR:
- Traditional definitions of Diplomacy privilege a realist lens of IR
- The problems with viewing Twitter Diplomacy from a realist lens
- The appropriateness of studying Twitter Diplomacy from a Constructivist lens

1.3 The curios case of the custom-made diplomatic practices:
- Distinct societies practiced distinct diplomatic practices
- Early diplomatic practices
- Al Jiwar in Arabian tribes
- Faith-based diplomatic missions

1.4 The evolution of modern day diplomacy:
- The establishment of the first MFA
- The expansion of the role of diplomacy
- The establishment of multilateral institutions
- The rise and spread of public diplomacy

1.5 The defining diplomatic practice of modern day: Twitter Diplomacy
- The rise of the Internet and SNSs
- The quick adoption of Twitter by the U.S state department
- The adoption of Twitter by most actors in IR
- The establishment of Digital Diplomacy units within MFAs in some states

All the Definitions

Diplomacy is an essential political activity that enables states to secure their objectives and interests without the resort to force, propaganda or the law (2). It is the art of state policy communication and representation (3). Even though traditional definitions of diplomacy are sometimes confused with foreign policy, they're not the same. Diplomacy is the main, but not only instrument of foreign policy (4). Foreign policy is the activity of furthering national interests and attempting to reshape the distribution of power in the international arena (4). In other words, diplomacy is the how, and foreign policy is the why. And hence Twitter Diplomacy could be (and often is) an extension of the outlined foreign policy goals of states. In so far as the deliberate Twitter Diplomacy of state-actors goes.

Public diplomacy, on the other hand is an extension of Diplomacy. While diplomacy is the attempt of influencing international relations through actor-to-actor contact, public diplomacy is the attempt of influencing international relations through actor-to-people contact (5). Only foreign people, though. Various definitions for public diplomacy have been proposed. In fact, it has been argued that Public Diplomacy is the most important political communication issue in the 21st century (6). Tuch proposed that Public Diplomacy is conducted to "bring about understanding for its nation's ideas and ideals, its institutions and culture, as well as its national goals and policies" (6). Tuch focuses on constructing a favorable image of the state. An important theme that emerges with Tuch's definition is that of 'understanding' of the particular viewpoints of the state. According to Malone and Fisher, building relationships with foreign publics is the key element of Public Diplomacy (6). This is at the backdrop of increasing ideals of democracy; where legitimacy of state and state policies are derived from the people, making 'the people' an important stakeholder in the sober act of politics and foreign policy design. Of course, this is not to say that only democratic states engage in public diplomacy. On the contrary, there are lots of non-democratic states that have well-constructed and executed public diplomacy programs. For instance, it was a 30-minute radio show that piloted on Cairo radio on the 4th of July 1953 called Sawt Al Arab that became the most powerful public diplomacy tool that allowed Nasserism to gain momentum across the entire Arab world (7) (8). Public diplomacy can be also be viewed as a country's attempts to exert as much control as possible over the framing of policies and political discourses to foreign publics (6). It seems that there is consensus on the main functions of public diplomacy: the construction of a favorable image, the communication with a foreign public and some kind of political gain from the constructed image.

Why Twitter Diplomacy necessitates a Constructivist lens of IR

The two definitions of Diplomacy that were introduced within the section above both are generally accepted as traditional definitions for Diplomacy. Similarly, both of those definitions emerged and served a realist lens of International Relations. Realism is one of three main schools of thought in International Relations. It is a lens of IR that views the relations between states as based on might, not right. Naturally, this theory paves the way to an emphasis on military might, security and the balance of powers between states. It also places 'the state' as the center of all interactions in International Relations. Exclusively. This discounts the role of internal factors within states that do have an influence on IR. Hence, realism struggles to account for the important influence of non-state actors as legitimate actors in the international arena. It also fails to give enough weight to the waves of change that cyclically emerge within societies, including changes in social attitudes, changes in global values, changes in identities of groups, or other changes that can and do alter discourses within and beyond states.

To offset the privileging of a realist vision, I make the following changes in both definitions respectively: Diplomacy is an essential political activity that enables ~~states~~ politically motivated entities to secure their objectives and interests without the resort to force, propaganda or the law, and diplomacy is the art of ~~state~~ policy communication and representation. The distinction between the state-centric and non-state-centric definition of diplomacy serves a very important purpose within the scope of this study. And the purpose is that Twitter Diplomacy in general mandates a more constructivist lens of analysis because of its very nature. Constructivism is a lens of IR that views international relations as ultimately shaped and reshaped by collective culture, group identities and shared norms and values. Its core belief is that actors in IR act according to a 'belief-system,' which is usually accepted as the 'norm' to some segment of local or global society. This belief system often emerges from persuasive ideas that spread across societies cyclically. To constructivists, this makes the main actors in IR the disseminators of the new persuasive ideas that often-become pillars of belief systems in entire societies. This also makes the main instrument of change within IR the newly formed persuasive ideas and the new values and norms they are trying to establish. Similarly, it makes the main change-makers the early communicators of the emerging norms, or 'norm entrepreneurs. Constructivism has helped in explaining the successes and failures that some promoters of new ideas have had in re-shaping values and norms.

Hence, Twitter Diplomacy necessitates a constructivist lens. At least initially. This is not only due to the nature of Twitter Diplomacy itself, as an exercise in idea expression and dissemination, but also because of the first users of Twitter Diplomacy who were non-state actors. As will be detailed in later sections, Twitter Diplomacy emerged as an experiment in change-making. At least so in an Arabic context. And hence an objective analysis of the conduct of Twitter Diplomacy cannot privilege a realist lens.

The curious case of the custom-made diplomatic practices

It is safe to say that Diplomacy is one of the most ancient practices developed by our societies, in response to other societies. It seems that there is evidence of Diplomatic practices by almost every civilization known to us. It is beyond my scope to trace the point zero of Diplomacy, a task I leave to Historians and romanticizing nationalist folklorists. Yet, what seems to be relevant is that Diplomacy had survived the dimensions of time and space. And of course, the entire spectrum of human cultures. At some point, societies unanimously concluded that it is a better idea to not shoot the messenger from the other side. Even the most orthodox realist societies concluded that there is at least *some* utility in diplomacy. Furthermore, within distinct communities, very distinct diplomatic practices came and went.

Some of the earlier Diplomatic practices known to us include the Amarna letters written on clay tablet from the Egyptian Dynasty to neighboring kingdom leaders in the 14th Century BCE (2). This collection of 382 clays gives us an insight to the Diplomatic practices of that time, including the fact that the letters were written in the language of Ancient Mesopotamia instead of that of ancient Egypt (2). Both the elaborate nature of the tablets, the contents within the tablet and the choice of language all show how intentional the act of diplomacy was to the Egyptian Dynasty. Additionally, multiple peace treaties have been found in 2100 BCE between Mesopotamia and other states including Lagash and Umma and an International peace treaty between Egyptian and Hiti in the 12th century BCE (2). Similarly, a common diplomatic practice within pre-Islamic Arabian tribes was the practice of extending 'Al Jiwar' to a person at risk of persecution (9). Al Jiwar is loosely translated to 'protection' or 'immunity' or even 'political asylum' in modern day political language. Extending 'Al Jiwar' or immunity to a member that is vulnerable to persecution sometimes by the tribe itself is synonymous to being under the protection of the member who extended the Jiwar. The honor code and kinship codes of conduct within the tribe places the expectation on all honorable members of the tribe to respect the extended Jiwar of the protector. Respecting the sanctity of the Jiwar is indicative of both the general 'honorability' of the members of the group and the social status of the protector (9). If the Jiwar is violated by members of the tribe (or non-members) then the extender of the Jiwar is expected to spare no efforts in protecting the person he claimed is under 'his protection.' Including the use of force. Otherwise, he risks losing his status, honor and the binding contract of his word (9). Al Jiwar diffused into and is still practiced within modern day Afghanistan and has become one of the main pillars of the Pashtunwali honor code system, called Nanawatay (10). The 'immunity' and protection extended to Al Qaeda by the Taliban is a text-book example of extending Al Jiwar, and going to war on their behalf, if attacked. Another example of community-specific diplomatic practices is the faith-based prophetic missions. For instance, in the Arabic language the title of the messenger literally translates into 'prophet.' Which makes the prophet ultimately a diplomat and the diplomat ultimately a prophet. A conviction that isn't exclusive to the Arabs. In fact, diplomatic studies' scholars seem to be in consensus that the first diplomatic missions were probably the prophetic missions (4).

Romantic as that may sound. God has long argued on behalf of Diplomacy, by practicing it routinely. This raised the status of the early 'prophet' and 'diplomat,' setting the ground for what would later become specific statuses and practices for diplomats.

It certainly seems that every point in time had very specific practices of diplomacy. Societies appear to custom-make their diplomatic practices, that don't necessarily translate well into a different time and place. This adds to the uniqueness of the emerged custom-made diplomatic practice because it appears to exist at very specific coordinates in space and time, adding another opportunity for researchers to extract useful information about the hidden and the implied codes and conducts within that community, that may have not been quite as obvious through examining different social activities for that community.

And so, in a way, it is very likely that today's Tweets could serve as tomorrow's Amarna letters.

The evolution of modern-day Diplomacy

Modern day Diplomacy can be traced back to the Italian peninsula in the 15th Century AD, diffusing into France and eventually admired and adopted by the British system as well (11). This was the basis of not only modern Diplomacy but also bilateral systems. By the 20th century, diplomacy expanded to not only encompass relations between two states bilaterally but also to regulate and communicate multilaterally with a collection of states (4).

In 1626, the French Chief Minister, the famous Cardinal Richelieu created the first Ministry of Foreign Affairs in modern History (11). It was his view that a resident ambassador is a necessity to maintain the balance of power in Europe and hence achieve stability for France and the European continent. The name stuck with most European states and MFAs were soon the standard state policy for Diplomatic communications (11). MFAs became sophisticated and bureaucratic. With every year that passed in the international system without total war, Diplomacy claimed a win. In 1796, Edmund Burke expanded the definition of Diplomacy to include activities such as gathering information, clarifying intentions and communicating good will (11). Clearly, diplomacy was being expanded to more than envoys and negotiations. As time and years-without-total-wars passed, Diplomacy became a political activity not left to the sidelines but became to be seen as an essential activity within the activity of politics, gaining more legitimacy, importance and efficacy in the eyes of practitioners. This became institutionalized not just at the state level but also the international level; states developed protocols, rules and regulations to set the standards for diplomacy at the international level. Exponentially, global diplomatic institutions like the UN gained more prestige and legitimacy in the international community. This was forming at the backdrop of a multipolar world increasingly accepting of the role of non-state actors in International Relations and a shift from Realism to Liberalism. In fact, during the outbreak of the Covid-19

Pandemic, the WHO became the first responder to the international crisis as an international crisis, the first to securitize (12) the pandemic with a securitization speech (13) and the most legitimate source of information to states. And the public, interestingly enough. A story worth exploring on a separate occasion.

Meanwhile, public diplomacy was coined by Edmund Gullion in 1965 as a replacement for the term 'propaganda,' because of the negative connotations to it (5). Cull argued that one of the main objectives of explicitly finding another name for what was traditionally known as propaganda was for American diplomats to be able to accuse Russia of using propaganda while denying that the U.S was doing the same, at the onset of the cold war (5). Indeed, he quoted that Senator Fulbright had referred to the public diplomacy office as a 'propaganda agency' while arguing to not transfer his cultural diplomacy program to the public diplomacy office (5). The term public diplomacy was not used outside of the states until the 1990s, in explaining the influence of the US in Eastern Europe (5). Initially, public diplomacy had relied on one-way communication (14). An expected feature of public diplomacy, where most large-scale communication methods were indeed one-way. Zaharna described this process as a linear process, with the goal of persuasion or control (14). In 2005, Zaharna proposed that Public Diplomacy should be more than just presentation and should include participation (6). Zaharna and Uysal argued that governments have indeed realized that they can no longer engage in traditional media relations, non-transparency and one-way messaging while remaining legitimate in the eyes of the stakeholders (15).

A Timeline of the Evolution of Diplomacy

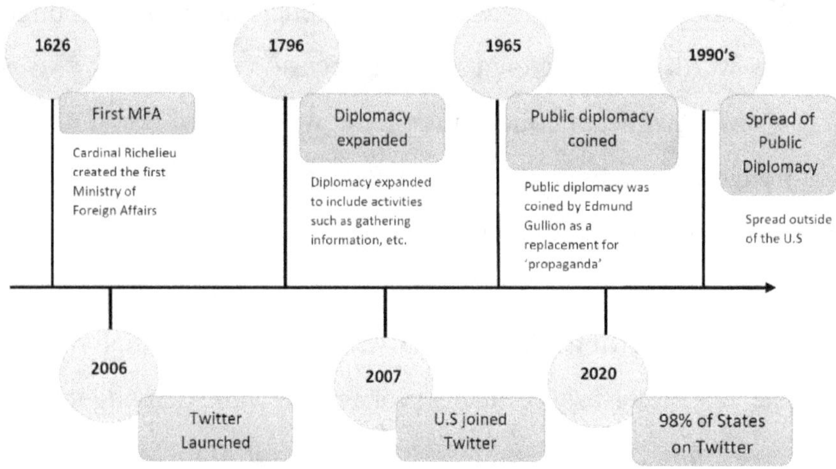

Figure 1 - The Evolution of Diplomacy

The defining diplomatic practice of modern day: Twitter Diplomacy

As the internet penetration rates increased and more people started using SNSs (social networking sites) in their daily lives, a lot of states identified this as an opportunity and were early adopters at institutionalizing digital diplomacy. Indeed, the adoption of SNSs to conduct diplomacy has been such a significant trend that it has been accepted as a 'paradigm shift' by scholars in the field (16). For example, the U.S. diplomatic establishment was among the first converts to digital platforms. As early as 2006 – the same year Twitter was launched, Secretary of State Condoleezza Rice talked about emerging technologies as "a great way to connect with millions of new people" around the world (Rice, 2006, para. 20). The U.S. State Department joined Twitter in October 2007 and, as of September 2019, had more than 5 million followers. Twitter somehow became the platform of choice for IR actors (3). By 2018, 97% of the UN member states were already on Twitter, confirming the undeniable trend (17). The latest Twiplomacy report reveals that 98% of UN member states are now on Twitter. This migration of state-actors I later call *the digital pilgrimage* and elaborate on in Chapter 2. Similarly, all recognized global institutions, NGOs and IGOs also established a solid Twitter presence (18). Twitter has been utilized by the pilgrims as a communication tool with fellow diplomats, engagement with the public, crisis management, mobilization, diaspora engagement, information gathering, a promotional tool, countering extremist narratives and for diplomatic prestige. The peculiar conduct of IR-actors on Twitter – Twitter Diplomacy – has become so normalized that it isn't unusual that state-actors announce official positions in a tweet or that individual tweets make their way routinely on national news. Indeed, digital diplomacy has become such an important diplomatic practice of the modern state that Australia created an Australian Ambassador for Cyber Affairs (19). Similarly, some states officially institutionalized Twitter Diplomacy, such as Israel, Britain and New Zealand which launched a digital diplomacy unit (20).The extent of the pervasiveness of Twitter Diplomacy calls for an urgent and comprehensive exploration of meaning encoded within the specific practices that have become standard twitter diplomacy policies of actors.

Conclusion

This chapter provided a brief overview of diplomacy. It provided definitions for diplomacy, foreign policy and public diplomacy and established that all of them are generally accepted as state-centric in the literature. It argued that Twitter Diplomacy, however, should be studied initially with a constructivist lens. It then provided a brief overview of early diplomatic practices and went on to follow the timeline of the evolution of diplomacy, highlighting important events. Finally, it established that the modern diplomatic practice of the current day is Twitter Diplomacy. In chapter 2, I examine how Twitter Diplomacy emerged.

Chapter 2:
Welcome to the Cyberspace – an Analytical overview of contemporary debates

Introduction

There's no such thing as a simple story. Sometimes stories are embedded within stories embedded within stories. This gives the story layers of complexities that opens its up for the possibility of a variety of interpretations. In the humanities, that's called multi-causality. Every academic investigation in the humanities is cursed with the complexity of the chased story being embedded within a story embedded within a story. No different is the story of Twitter Diplomacy. The story of Twitter Diplomacy is embedded within the story of Diplomacy and within the Internet, yet is much more than the product of the two of them (figure 2).

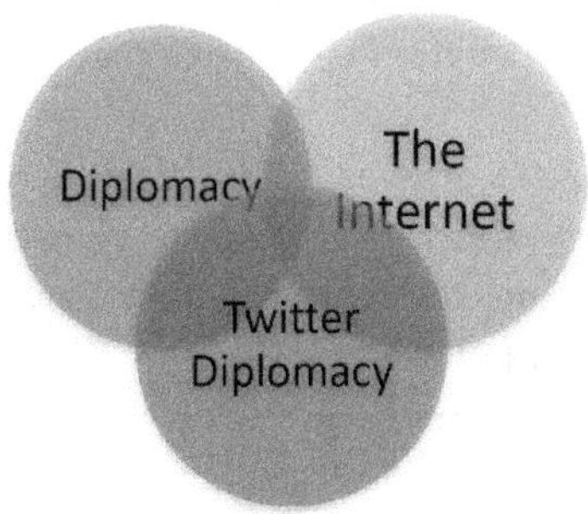

Figure 2 - Twitter Diplomacy Illustration

Twitter Diplomacy doesn't exist in a void. To understand the action-patterns within Twitter and the implications of Twitter Diplomacy for states and people, a brief investigation on the medium that exists within is certainly called for. This is because the medium itself imposes a few embedded laws that are equivalent to the physical laws in the parallel, physical human experience. At least, engaging reflexively with some of the meta-questions about the current format and implications of the cyberspace allows us to get a little closer towards mapping what is general to the Internet, what is specific to Twitter Diplomacy and what overlaps both of them.

Objectives:

2.1 Why we should explore the explore feeds:

- The flaws of cyberspace in its current form
- Challenging the notion of the inherent 'goodness' of connectivity
- Establishes that cyberspace played an undefined role in the development of various IR events in the past two decades
- Argues why we should – as academics – explore the ecosystems of the politicized social media platforms with seriousness and vigour

2.2 The political weaponization of social media:

- Establishes that there is virtually no regulation within cyberspace in general and by extension social media
- Outlines the difficulties in proposing regulations within cyberspace
- Examines the idea of social media as weapons
- Argues why the American experience with social media political weapons is unique and hence will have consequences on global efforts for cyber policies

2.3 Arms control treaty for social media:

- Outlines who are the stakeholders who should be considered for such a treaty
- Provides an overview on who the current stakeholders are in the way the cyberspace operates
- Introduces the concepts of deep fakes, international crime depositories and internet watch dogs

2.4 Regulating social media at home:

- Introduces the concept of digital sovereignty
- Discusses how increased connectivity controls the outcomes of some events
- Examines how some governments are establishing digital sovereignty
- Examines legal challenges for regulating Tech platforms
- Examines the moral challenges of allowing Tech platforms to regulate content on cyberspace
- Discusses the challenge of social media illiteracy of lawmakers
- Introduces the debate of Internet rights

2.5 Does the Internet alter IR:

- Examines the two main arguments on the effect of the Internet on IR
- Discusses how cyberspace allows the extension of life for authoritarianism
- Introduces the idea of digital authoritarianism as a competitor with liberal democracy
- Discusses how states will be categorized according to the openness and closeness of their internet
- Examines the rich history of disruptive communication technologies

Why we should explore the 'explore feeds'

The idea of a 'global village' was theorized by media theorist Marshal McLuhan (21). In an almost prophetic stroke, McLuhan prophesized a world where anyone is connecting to anyone, and anyone is connecting to everyone and everyone is connecting to everyone. All at the same time. And *all* the time. This was a global village that is multi-ethnic, multi-racial, multi-cultural, multi-lingual, multi-spatial, multi-temporal, multi-religious, multi-polar and certainly not flat. Implied in this prophecy is the judgment that a connected, communicating world is inherently a good thing. The idea was that if everyone was speaking to everyone, good things will happen. And so natural was the implication, that it was widely accepted as a given. Virtually no body challenged the notion that multi-layers of communication occurring at real-time *and* the same time that completely bypass national borders as though they were lines of smoke (or perfume) was in fact a good thing. Until the chaos simmering within the cyberspace leaked into the order of the human space; challenging state-actors, scholars and the average user on the inherent 'goodness' of cyberspace in its current form of existence and mode of operation. Suddenly, the question of the inherent goodness of everyone communicating with everyone came under scrutiny. In recent years one strange event after the other has led researchers to question the correlation, *complicity* or *causality* of the Internet in relation to these events. As Eva Williams, one of the founders of Twitter was quoted to have said "I thought once everybody could speak freely and exchange information and ideas, the world is automatically going to be a better place. I was wrong about that" (22). Some of the events we've seen where the Internet played a role of an undefined magnitude were revolutions, civil wars, political polarizations, disinformation campaigns, terrorist organizations' recruitment campaigns, diplomatic communications, social movements, radicalizations, proliferation of hate speech and hate crime incitements, interference in the internal matters of a sovereign state and who knows what else (as will be detailed in the sections to come).

Our understanding of how the Internet operates in general and how it affects us is still in its infancy. However, just because we don't understand something doesn't mean we can deny it. In fact, there's plenty of scholarly arguments that hypothesize that all knowledge is identified inductively. According to Dr. Jordan Peterson, people act out the law first, then the law becomes the body of law as we know it second. This same scholarly hypothesis was articulated by Rumsfeld in a simple and memorable statement: there's the known known and there's the *known unknown* (23). Internet is currently our known unknown. Our task, as scientists, was to leave a margin of space for what we didn't know and what we *kind of* know about this Internet during its infancy. Now, our job has evolved to fill in this margin of space, by asking the reflexive, critical and contemplative questions about the current structure of the Internet. And only after understanding these laws can some states who have already invested in extensive (yet not necessarily well-informed) Twitter Diplomacy efforts hope to begin changing them to deliberate policies. And by extension develop some level of predictability and stability in the role that the Internet will continue to play in future events.

The Political Weaponization of social media

Even though any human community (real or imagined) is expected to have a little bit of chaos and a little bit of order embedded in it, the cyber space- in its current form - seems to be disproportionately skewed towards the chaotic side. The question is: how much chaos can a mutually constructed fictional world handle before descending into absolute anarchy? This is inherently a question of regulating the Internet – a proposal that has been articulated by a variety of different international actors. Yet, most actors did not engage in precise language in specifying what they viewed as currently problematic (and whether it was human-centric or state-centric) and hence they failed at specifying what needs to be regulated in cyber space. The vagueness of the proposition disallowed researchers from zeroing in on what Internet regulations of an international order could attempt to regulate.

Interestingly, when the only surviving super power in the world (at the time of writing this paper) seriously debates foreign interference in its 2016 elections by an old rival through cyber space, the U.S and the media formulate a question that does contain a clear dimension that has been identified as problematic in its current form and hence could be regulated. The question is: has the Internet become a weapon of serious consequence? Indeed, the political weaponization of specifically social media has been a hot topic in international relations, after Russia's alleged meddling in the United States' electoral process. And no wonder. Democratic standards really, *really* shame nations. Hence, it is only natural that anything that undermines a democratic process is framed as a weapon. This is not said that there is anything new about either election meddling or in general interference in a sovereign state's internal matters. On the contrary, all states have participated in some form of an eccentric espionage attempt against another state. For instance, during the Cold War, Russia claimed that the CIA was the source of the HIV virus and that Russia was responsible for the 'assassination' of President John F. Kennedy, while the US and the UK engaged in ambitious anti-communist programs that can only be described as propaganda and exported them to Italy and Chile, among others (24). What is novel about meddling through the internet is the ability to do that at scale covertly on a platform that is vibrating with unregulated content, unverified users, uncategorized spyware and many tweets. For instance, so grave was the perceived threat of the covertness of the political weaponization of social media that the FBI Director felt the need to directly address and warn the American public – a move that completely contradicts a long tradition of a bureaucracy cloaked with secrecy. An additional example that clearly demonstrates political weaponization of social media is the incident that has been called 'the tale of two rallies' in Houston, Texas, where a group of protestors gathered in front of an Islamic center. Some of the protestors believed they were protesting for

Texas's secession from the union, while others believed they were attending a rally for United Muslims of America (25). Both groups were inspired to attend through Facebook posts (25). After congressional investigation by Special Counsel Robert Mueller, the confusion was attributed to a company called the Internet Research Agency – a Russian linked troll farm (25). The intention behind the deliberate confusion constructed was to pit Americans against each other, the investigations revealed (25). Similarly, a remarkable study by Jonathan Albright, a Professor at Columbia University masterfully detailed how the same agency – the Internet Research agency – spread propaganda, misinformation and extreme viewpoints by visibly distorting and misinterpreting information from the mainstream media (26). A more recent example is China's disinformation campaign during the initial phases of the covid-19 crises, directed at sowing chaos and panic in the United States by spreading disinformation warning that then President Donald Trump is planning on installing a two-week national lockdown mid-march (27). It seems that the panic ripples were so pervasive that the National Security Council felt the unusual need to actually Tweet that this was false information (27).

The United States wasn't by any means the first state to realize that social media has been weaponized, yet its recognition of the weaponization of social media will produce a novel and global increment in policy maker's consciousness for two reasons. First, the United States remains in a unique position historically as the world's only super power. Hence, its influence to shape global agendas in International Relations will remain extraordinarily high. Second, the U.S has long positioned itself as the chief negotiator on behalf of Liberal Democracy, in the global battle of value systems. So, to have the world's (perceived) ideal democracy be vulnerable to online political weapons has serious theoretical consequences in IR. In fact, there's actually been plenty of evidence for the political weaponization of social media in progressive, authoritarian and developing states. Take for instance, the Ethiopian diaspora's persistent online disinformation campaigns aimed at fueling the Ethiopian public's legitimate discontent with the government by spreading false information about the government, hoping for mobilization against it (28). Russia was also accused of the 15% Twitter activity that was generated by bots, all of which supported far-right candidates in Italy's elections (24). While in Macedonia, a plethora of new Twitter accounts proliferated 40 days before the national referendum for renaming the country, also attributed to the Kremlin (24). Increased bot activity was reported in the lead up to national elections across multiple different states including Bosnia, Sweden and Herzegovina (24). Similarly, in Mexico a spurge of content discrediting presidential candidate Andres Manual Lopez surfaced the Internet originating from Iran, Argentina, Venezuela and Russia (24). Furthermore, it is actually undisputed in literature now that Internet was adopted by state-actors initially to counter extremist ideologies by terrorist groups, which could be argued were the first to weaponize social media and hence effectively monopolized it for a while. Hence the United States was long aware of the possibility of politically weaponizing social media and cyber space. After all, it was America that invented the Internet in the first place. Yet, based on the magnitude of the shock to the 2016 electoral meddling expressed by American state-actors and the American public, it seems that the United States – and possibly the entire world – were under the impression that democracies were somewhat immune to online political weapons. A perfectly reasonable conclusion at a time where research on social media was mostly focused on its role in revolutions, which mostly demanded democracy (or something that resembles it), and framed tech platforms as democracy accelerators. Certainly not democracy decelerators. Hence, the bursting of the bubble of immunity of democracies from online political weapons is bound to have ripples of increments in consciousness of states across the world on the extent of the potency of the political weaponization of social media.

Arms control treaty for social media

Those who were long observant of how social media was weaponized proposed the extension of existing arms control regulations to include the Internet or the drafting of new international treaties that regulate Internet as a weapon. In a 2015 joint press conference, then Chinese President Xi Jinping and American President Barack Obama announced that the two states would work together to produce international rules for appropriate conduct on the Internet (29). Any comprehensive framework that will be proposed to attempt to regulate the Internet as a weapon will inevitably have to include non-state actors as legitimate stakeholders. The more traditional non-state actors that will have to be a part of this framework will be the same IGOs that the overwhelming majority of the international community has increasingly accepted as legitimate actors in the world order, such as the U.N. Yet, any efforts towards furthering an arms control treaty for the Internet would quickly run into the problem of the new power configuration of the Internet that is not a mirror image of real life power configurations, which allowed the emergence of powerful non-state stakeholders (that aren't multilateral institutions) in cyberspace that were not previously seen as legitimate stakeholders in International Relations; Multinational Corporations. Of course, MNCs have had a long history of influencing international affairs and foreign policy. For instance, the 1953 British coup engineered in Iran was mainly to protect British petroleum companies' interest (30). Yet, historically the ability of MNCs to influence foreign policy and international affairs was the exception, not the norm, and was mainly achieved through lobbying respective governments. Certainty not the reverse. Never before have they emerged as active players in international affairs of such magnitude. For example, at the time of the writing of this paper, Twitter had permanently suspended the account of former President Donald Trump after the Capitol Hill incident (31), whereas YouTube and Facebook temporarily shut them down (32). It is true that Twitter has been engaged in multiple rounds of cleaning efforts, removing millions of fake accounts from its platforms, but never has it de-platformed a world leader. This unprecedented deplatforming of a major state-actor produced a wave of media releases by state-actors expressing worry at tech companies' unprecedented ability and power to shape public discourses. Or more accurately, the newly found *acceptability* and expectation of tech companies to do so. Somehow tech policies became public policies. Currently, this acceptability and expectation have only been expressed by American publics and lawmakers, but what if these sentiments spill over across borders to become universally recognized expectations from tech companies? One of the most outspoken state-actors expressing worry about the new magnitude of the role of tech companies in shaping domestic and international politics was German chancellor Angela Merkel, who was actually one of the voices calling on tech companies to moderate political content on their platforms just a few years ago (33). The German chancellor was calling for moderation, not alteration of political discourse. Apparently. Similarly, India's Narendra Modi, Brazil's Jair Bolsonaro, and the Philippine's Rodrigo Duterte are all right wing elected leaders who have used tech platforms extensively to communicate directly with their support bases and have all been accused of exasperating divisions with their respective societies, attacking independent journalists and inciting hate speech (33). A damning UN report found that

Facebook was used extensively to spread and mobilize hate that contributed to the ethnic cleansing of Rohingyan Muslims (34). How would content moderation look for them, post-Trump detweeting? Non-American state actors *should* very much be worried because of the unclear metrics of the new and abstract red line that tech companies considered President Donald Trump to have crossed. State-actors are asking important questions about the mandate of tech companies to pass judgment and extend influence on what is now seen as public-private-national space. This new paradigm shift guarantees tech companies a seat in the discussions leading to an Internet controls treaty.

Another group of non-traditional actors that we should be expecting to see as a part of the discussion are mass surveillance companies. Big data companies that sell sophisticated surveillance technology to state-actors and criminal organizations, alike, have existed for a long time. One such company is NSO – an Israeli company that is known to have sold to authoritarian regimes sophisticated mass surveillance equipment. There is absolutely no accountability for mass digital surveillance companies currently. This has allowed for major abuses and misuses by state-actors and criminal organizations, allowing companies to sell one state's citizen information to a foreign state, enabling meddling in the internal affairs of a sovereign state. For example, it was a California-based company that sold to the Assad regime his own citizens' data that allowed for identifying and cracking down on the dissenters.

Some states are not just aware of the power of surveillance companies, but are highly distrustful of who could be surveilling their citizens. For instance, Russia passed a bill that requires its citizens' data to be stored only on Russian soil (35). Furthermore, some have suggested the construction of independent organizations that monitor transactions of mass surveillance companies. A comprehensive framework for a cyberspace weapons control treaty should include these mass surveillance companies, extending legal frameworks for regulating the flow of citizens' data between sovereign states.

A third group of non-state actors that are expected to emerge during the discussions are international depositories – or watch dogs – for criminal digital evidences. Videos of major human right's violations routinely circulate on social media, fueling the debate on whether tech companies should introduce a policy that disallows these sensitive and graphic images to casually find their homes on users' newsfeeds. One side argues that exposing violations increases the visibility of some crimes and thus helps bring the aggressors to justice. This side is often embraced by activists, NGOs and human rights organizations. This side also argues that this is one of the major functions of social media. The other side, however, argues that routinely allowing graphic, sensitive crime videos to circulate within news feeds either desensitizes audiences to violence or plays a critical role in recruiting for terrorist organizations. Furthermore, the emerging trend of deep fakes – technology that allows the engineering of high-quality fake content that is very difficult to detect – is an additional problem that allows the Internet to be a hub for misinformation. A novel case where digital evidence was used to indict a criminal proved the utility and acceptability of digital evidence in delivering justice is in the Libyan X's case – who was accused of war crimes. This produces a need to hold on to all criminal records, since the Law is extending admissibility to digital evidence now. Because anything that you tweet can be and will be used against you.

Regulating social media at Home

How the Internet operates *within* states is a different issue. There are three main, non-exhaustive issues within the regulation of the Internet within national boundaries that I will examine. First is the question of digital sovereignty. Second is jurisdiction. And third is rights.

The first question of digital sovereignty is within the same wavelength of disallowing political foreign intervention within the internal matters of a sovereign state through the weaponization of cyber space. Yet, it is more reflexive and theoretical than an arms control treaty. It is a much more contemplative exploration of what it means traditionally to be sovereign and what it specifically means to be digitally sovereign in a networked cyber space. Digital sovereignty is synonymous with Joshua Ramo's 'hard gate-keeping' – which calls for shifting the dynamics of Westphalian sovereignty to maintain networked sovereignty (36). In practice, digital sovereignty was first (ironically) proposed in a Bill by Russia, allegedly to allow it to cut off some parts of Russia from the rest of the world (37). This Bill allows the Russian government to control the flow of information and communication to and from citizens, by requiring service providers to produce reports on how they direct traffic to Russians (37). This allows Russia to monitor and control all information entering its borders or leaving its border, hence is inherently anti-globalist. Or selectively globalist. Service providers are also expected to install special equipment as required by the government (37). In addition to the proposed digital sovereignty bill, Russia passed laws that criminalize posting fake news or offending the government on social media platforms (37). Thus, the Kremlin is looking to centralize both the content and structure of how the Internet operates within its borders (37). The idea is to allow the government to block or remove any content that it deems harmful to the stability of the state and to cut-off the Internet during times of crises (37). In fact, Russia has already implemented its plan of controlling connectivity in times of crises. In 2019, Ingushetia agreed on redrawing its borders with its neighbor, Chechnya. The deal involved a land swap. Protests erupted protesting the land swap. The Internet was cut off for 2 weeks in October to curtail communication and hence further escalation (37). Similarly, On March 16, there was a meeting of local activists in Ingushetia, where the same happened. The internet was cut off across the region until the meeting ended (37). Russia is one of the very few countries where local tech companies is more popular than foreign tech companies. The local tech companies in Russia are all private enterprises that were built without any help from the government. Russian tech companies were vocal publicly about their resistance to the proposed digital sovereignty bill proposed by the government and the attempts to extend more influence on the content within their platforms. Yet, in January of 2019, they accepted the Bill, after the government promised to pay for new equipment. Roskomsvoboda – is Russia's only internet watchdog. It believes that communication can be centralized and directed from the Kremlin for some services like YouTube, but cannot be done for all services and all parts of Russia. The new law may damage the internet infrastructure in Russia and lower the internet speed in Russia and has already damaged Russian companies' future business opportunities in other countries. Some International tech companies also reluctantly accepted Russia's new attempts at changing the rules within its borders, including EBay, PayPal and booking.com. Other states have also attempted to enact a less comprehensive, but similar policy objectives to Russia's Digital sovereignty policy. They have tried to control the flow and content of information. For example, the Ethiopian government restricted access to the internet in response to the October 9 upheaval after it declared a 6-month state of emergency (28). It increased internet blackouts and blocked access to social media platforms such as Facebook and Twitter (28). Ireland, the Czech Republic and Switzerland are all debating legislation that bans fake news on Internet platforms (24). Iran has similarly attempted to control some of the content on the Internet within its territory by sporadically blocking Twitter after the dubbing of the 2009 green movement as the 'twitter revolution' (wrongly so). Other states have blocked VPNs and encrypted texting platforms such as Telegram. The most cited example of attempting to control the content of Internet within national boundaries is China's infamous firewall, often dubbed as 'China's great Firewall.' It seems that some states have concluded that indeed it was a mistake to assume that multi-way connectivity was an inherently good thing.

Second, jurisdiction over tech companies within national borders remains a highly contentious topic for contemplation for law makers. Most tech giants are American companies. Yet, American users make up less than 5% of the total user base of American tech companies. This highlights the clear stakes of American tech giants in maintaining their user base, across borders. For example, in April 2017, Germany passed a law that fines tech companies up to 50 million Euros for not acting swiftly enough to tackle hate speech or illegal content (38). A broad coalition of opposition protested the legislation, which argued that the law privatizes law enforcement to tech companies. The coalition stated that German law should contravene what hate speech is, not social media companies. It is unclear what tech companies' starting position was on the responsibility to curb hate speech and extremist ideologies, especially with its lacking track record with terrorist organizations' use of social media platforms that went not only unmoderated but largely undetected for a substantial amount of time. But it does appear that the current position of some Tech giants is to gladly accept the responsibility of covering for a function usually monopolized by the body of the Law pre-cyber space. To allow automated algorithms to police morality – at scale - deserved a proper national debate (at least) before absent-mindedly nodding to social media companies to take it away. A second layer of analysis for the complexities of assigning social media companies with the task of policing morality is the obvious conflict of interest arising from the fact that tech companies are first and foremost businesses looking for economic gains. Still further, a third layer of analysis is the ideological exploration of what it means for a platform to become the co-author of messages. For example, Microsoft launched its Defending Democracy program which prevents online hacking, provides greater transparency for political advertising and explores technological solutions to protect elections and reduce meddling (24). Similarly, Twitter has been engaged in numerous clean-up spurges and both Twitter and Facebook have moderated content extensively over the last couple of years. Additionally, it is not clear which courts have jurisdiction over tech companies operating within foreign states, because sometimes they run their operations from a different location. For example, in 2016 a German court refused to accept a case by a German lawyer against Facebook because it was carrying out all its European operations from Ireland

(38). Another example of complicated jurisdiction is Wikipedia's decision to leave Turkey all-together after demands from Turkey from tech companies to remove content it deems sensitive in a post-failed-coup environment (34). An odd yet seriously consequential problem that arises with the topic of jurisdiction over tech companies is the limit of the understanding of politicians and law makers of how social media actually works, let alone identifying vulnerabilities in this sophisticated collection of nodes and signals that may compromise or stabilize democratic values. So even if we were able to clearly associate jurisdiction on tech companies to a specific national or multi-national court, we'd be left with the problem of social media illiteracy of juries. This was clearly evident in the almost embarrassing congressional hearing of Facebook's Mark Zuckerberg testifying for his company's role in the 2016 alleged election meddling, where congressman (X) asked simplistic questions about the business model of Facebook that incited laughter by some of the audiences, highlighting the extent of the disconnect between Silicon Valley and Washington. This raises a very simple but serious question about the law and social media companies: how do will the judges be able to tell if a law has been broken in cyber-space? In an environment where politicians, lawmakers and law enforcers are no match for the Internet literacy of a pre-teen, how are we supposed to trust that they will be able to identify a problem when it does present itself?

Third, is the question of rights. Internet has become the new promise of the free world. In 2018, President Donald Trump announced his National Cyber strategy, which calls for the need to extend internet freedom to all citizens of the world and to lament internet connectedness as an unnegotiable human right. President Donald Trump wasn't the first to propose the importance of the extradition of human rights to cyber space. He defined internet freedom as the ability to exercise all enshrined human rights in cyber space. Obviously, this is the counter-digital-sovereignty argument. And it only makes sense that the former rivals in the bipolar world champion opposing value-structures that are exact acronyms to each other. In fact, the internet freedom league has long been proposed by (X). Similarly, in 1997, political activist John Perry Barlow published his 'Declaration of independence of cyber space' inherently arguing for the construction of an Internet where rights are preserved. The debate on whether or not internet freedom is a fundamental human right and its trajectory to be formerly included in the treaty for social, economic and political rights could further provoke important questions in IR like: would a state or a coalition of states extend the concept of R2P to states that violate the Internet freedoms of their citizens?

Does the Internet alter IR?

There are two main arguments on the influence of the Internet on International Relations. Some argue that the Internet has altered the conduct, structure and theories of International Relations to such a significant degree that there is little reason to believe that any new technology in the future would be able to produce a paradigm shift of the magnitude that has been witnessed with the emergence of cyber space. For example, the Internet has allowed states to exert an unprecedented level of control and conformity, as is apparent in China's infamous social credit system, which collects data on citizens online and offline and gives each citizen a 'score,' which is then utilized to rank his/her favorability for economic, social and legal mobility. Similarly, China has trained 36 governments to develop their own citizen surveillance technology, according to Freedom House. The data that's available to authoritarian states along with continuous progression in AI produces algorithms which profile citizens that are most *likely* to dissent against their government. The magnitude and quality of the data that's available to authoritarian states combined with powerful algorithms has given authoritarianism an extension of life. It has allowed the propping up of a governance that should have probably died by now. Especially because of the emergence of what was dubbed as a democracy accelerator; social media platforms. Similarly, Marc Lynch wrote in 2011 that social media platforms will produce an ambiguous effect on authoritarian regimes (39). He further argued that networked communication fundamentally challenges the hierarchal nature of the nation-state (39). In fact, he even wrote an essay recommending further research on the adaptability of authoritarian states to networks. So noteworthy was the potency of some social media platforms, to some policy makers that it has prompted Mark Pfielfe, a former national security Advisor to argue that Twitter specifically should be nominated for a Nobel peace prize, for its role in Iran's Green movement in 2009 (40). The perceived influence of social media platforms for political organization by state-actors is also apparent in Russia's conviction that every protest that emerged in Russia or a historically Russian-friendly neighboring state were only made possible by social media platforms like Facebook and Twitter, and were guided by American sponsorship (37). In 2018, Wright wrote a very interesting argument predicting what he called as 'digital authoritarianism' as the new competitor to liberal democracy; because it allows for sustainable economic growth while still allowing a level of control on citizens that liberal democracy has long outgrown (41). He outlines that AI allows for selective censorship, allowing communication that will secure economic and civil gains, but disallowing flow of communication that is categorized as political by some states (41). Combined with access to citizen information from multiple platforms, it allows states to shape wanted and unwanted citizen behavior. On the same wavelength was an argument articulated by Alec Ross, a technology expert, that states will be categorized according to their openness or closeness with regards to their internet freedom for citizens. Anne Marie-Slaughter further argues that states that are more open will succeed more than states that exert a more closed internet society (36).

On the other hand, some scholars dispute the uniqueness of the Internet in International Relations and argue that those who believe the Internet altered IR in an unprecedented way discount the long history that communication technologies had on political discourse. Most notable of which in modern times is the effect that the printing press had in bringing about the age of enlightenment and propagating messages of Martin Luther that brought about the Protestant revolution at the turn of the millennium. Historian Robert Dartntorn wrote that "The marvels of communication technology in the present have produced a false consciousness about the past—even a sense that communication has no history, or had nothing of importance to consider before the days of television and the Internet." (40). The idea is that the Internet is just the latest disruptive communication technology added to a long line of disruptive communication technologies that cyclically emerge every now and whenever. Similarly, scholars have disputed the role of social media in organizing Iran's green movement on the basis that most of the content on Twitter during the movement were overwhelmingly produced in the English language and not Farsi, indicating that it wasn't used by locals to organize or communicate. Similarly, the role of social media in igniting and fueling the Arab uprisings – a long held popular conviction – was disproved (42). The conviction on this end is that the effect of the Internet has been greatly exaggerated and argue that every communication technology brings with it a few structural and novel changes in the way messages diffuse, but not so much so that IR is altered.

Conclusion

Cyberspace is equivalent to an inhabitable planet. And Twitter to one state within that planet. And so, in a lot of ways, attempting to understand one state without understanding the broader context of its existence seems incomplete. Unfortunately, our level of understanding of this broader context itself is very close to our level of understanding of Twitter Diplomacy; which is very basic. Hence, the questions that are being raised about the way Twitter Diplomacy works aren't very likely to be answered by the way the cyberspace generally works. However, that does not take away from the importance of engaging with meta-questions about networked communication, digital sovereignty, social media as political weapons, the law and social media, morality and social media, digital authoritarianism and open and closed internet societies for guiding our investigation on Twitter Diplomacy. Even if we have to do it simultaneously. Because a lot of the meta-questions about cyberspace could have a direct effect of Twitter Diplomacy. For instance, if tech platforms are accepted as political weapons in a legal capacity, then average users who post anything that can be interpreted as political would be an indictable crime. Such legal acceptance of social media as political weapons will then raise important questions about what qualifies certain content as 'political' and what doesn't? And who gets to decide, the users' state of citizenship or the state that perceives the posts as undermining its ‘political stability’? Similarly, if the international community was successful in outlining an arms control treaty for social media, does that mean political activity within Tech platforms qualifies as acts of international terrorism that allows for international action? Another example would be if states introduce legislation that criminalizes fake accounts, then an entire generation of social media users would be casually branded as criminals. The evolution of cyber policies naturally has an important effect on the conduct of Twitter Diplomacy and beyond. And hence, an eye on the general cyber narrative seems crucial for approaching the topic of Twitter Diplomacy.

Chapter 3:

The Arab Twittersphere is the heir of the neglected Arab Blogosphere

Introduction

The present Arab Twittersphere is so rooted in the past Arab blogosphere. Somewhere within the black hole of the Internet still exists knowledge that has yet to be unpacked. This is not to discount the many, many scholarly productions that did advance our

Chapter objectives:

3.1 Where it all started – the neglected Arab Blogosphere:

- The emergence of the Arab Blogosphere
- Norm entrepreneurs were the gatekeepers to the Arab Blogosphere
- The emergence of an online civic sphere to make up for the lack of an offline one
- A small readership. A subtle chain reaction.

3.2 The Arab Spring and the Emergence of the Arab Twittersphere:

- Enter social media
- From blogs to mini-blogs
- Norm entrepreneurs cascade the messages on social media
- A large readership. A big chain reaction.

3.3 The Arab Digital Pilgrimage:

- State-actors' adoption of Twitter Diplomacy was not an action, but a reaction to the realization of the potency of social media
- Arab state-actors steadily adopted Twitter

knowledge on the Arab blogosphere. But it is to say that in the darkness of the Internet, a lot of the answers are still hidden waiting to be extracted by the right questions. Chapter 3 attempts to narrate to the reader how the current Arab Twittersphere steadily emerged. The chapter examines some of the key factors and events that aided the rise of the Arab Twittersphere.

Where it all started: The neglected Arab blogosphere

The first blogs in the Arab world were established in the 1990s, where they grew steadily in the 2000s (Momani, 2015). Blogs were online journals with one slight twist: they were public. It seems that these unsponsored blogs were able to dent their societies, one blogpost at a time. Indeed, the emergence of the Arab blogosphere (and more importantly its consequences) forced a shift from the long tradition of the realist lens used to analyze the region to a more constructivist lens. This is because of the emergence of new norms. Norm alterations within a society takes place in three stages: (1) norm emergence, where the norm entrepreneurs engage in persuasion attempts to recruit more adopters of the new norm, (2) norm cascade, where the norm succeeds in finding adopters in a society, and (3) norm internalization, where the norm becomes a natural part of the identity of a society (43). It is widely accepted that the early bloggers were indeed norm entrepreneurs. In his book, Marc Lynch argued that the cyber space offered the cyber community in the Arab world an opportunity to carve out a new public sphere (44). Where none existed before, of course. A Harvard

University study estimated that there were 35,000 blogs in the Arab blogosphere in 2009 (45). Two major factors stood out in these blogs: a) 75% of the bloggers were below the age of 35 and b) the majority of bloggers used their own names (45). The first factor is attributed to the fact that there existed a well-documented 'youth bulge' in the Arab world during that time. In fact, it is estimated that 20% of the Arab population were categorized as 'youth' in 2010 (45). The Second factor can be attributed to Momani's implication that the new Arab youth population were looking to defy the social contract between their governments, just as they attempted to defy the authority of the more traditional elements in their communities (45). A constructivist analysis worth much more consideration than it received in literature, in my estimation. Some of the key blogs during the golden age of the Arabic blogosphere include Egypt's *Sand monkey*, Iraq's *Baghdad Burning*, Jordan's *Black Iris* and Tunisia's *Tunisian Girl,* to name just a few (45). As a millennial myself, I grew up following almost all of these blogs. What was evident in all of these blogs is: a) they gave an uncensored, almost careless account of 'life on the grounds'; including the dull, ordinary life of the average person in some corner of the Arab world, b) they managed to attract similar-minded audiences and form bubbles of almost-communities, and c) they thought no one cared. Lynch further argues that one of the main objectives of this new carved out space is to dig out information about governments and spread them to the public (44). Meaning: spring or no spring, they were normalizing the utilization of cyberspace to discuss and spread updates about governments. And because the cyber space community in the Arab world was so successful in normalizing this new-found objective, the more common expectation is that this newfound objective wasn't going anywhere. It came to stay. Hence, there was an element of journalism and norm-entrepreneurship right from the beginning within the blogosphere. This was the first time where news broadcasting wasn't exclusively controlled by a few dynasties, opinions didn't have to be politically correct, and last names didn't matter very much. It leveled the playing field between the ones in power and the ones behind a screen in an unprecedented way. Indeed in 2013, the Dubai School of Government estimated that 25% of the Arab population visited blogs daily, 24% visited blogs several times a week and 17% did several times a day (45). The blogs were no Facebook, no one's disputing that. The follower base or the 'virality' of even the most followed blogs was much more limited than the most average current day 'social media influencer.' And that was only natural. This was because of the nature of blogging; they were extensive pieces of literature sometimes. In fact, I had the great pleasure of meeting one of the very few researchers in the field of communications who did original research on the Arab blogosphere and analyzed them. Dr. Samah demonstrated that the Arab blogs were in fact literary journalism (46). Because of the richness, length and literary quality of the blogs they attracted a few loyal readers (compared to modern-day social media literary journalists). Yet, it seems that these norm entrepreneurs were the silent soldiers who were able to disseminate and popularize new values to their small audiences, who were emboldened and propagated the norms even further. Enter social media.

The Arab Spring and the Emergence of the Arab Twittersphere

The trajectory of the Internet – in general – follows an incredibly steep inclination. So, before the academics were able to identify the game of blogs, there was a new, more gripping game: the game of social media. For instance, one study revealed that there were half a million new Twitter users each day in March of 2011. SNSs became the new WordPress and blogpost. Facebook allowed people to almost-blog without any limits on the characters and Twitter – of course – became the 140-character mini blogging site and the natural heir to the Arab blogosphere. Norm entrepreneurs were able to harness much more attention on these new-found almost-blogs than on the traditional ones, because of the newfound entertainment value of social media platforms. Simply put, people were already there. This new civic, social space combined with the decreasing costs of cellphones and the penetration of mobile data created an added opportunity for norm entrepreneurs. It is also worth noting that securing the attention of readers for a few seconds on a platform with heavy footfall is a much easier task than securing the attention of readers for a considerable amount of time on a platform with a considerably low(er) footfall. Which is why it is important we reopen the archives and study the Arab blogosphere further; as they are the original manifesto of the Arab cyber civic space. The final result was a very active civic community, where tech platforms where routinely used to establish and mobilize support for campaigns. One such campaign was Wael Ghonim's 'We are all Khaled Said' Facebook group, which published a cell-phone picture of a mutilated Khaled Said, a student who witnessed the illegal transaction of a police officer who was pulled out of an Internet café and beaten to death (45). Another influential campaign in Egypt was Asma Mahfouz's video blogs, where she infused calls to protests with notions of honor and nationalism (45). An unusual combination that proved very effective. In Saudi Arabia, Waleed Abu Al Khair initiated a bold twitter campaign with the title 'the salary is not enough' – in Arabic – that generated 17 million responses, while Loujain Hathloul took to Twitter to voice her dissatisfaction with practices, she considered discriminatory against women (45). Similarly, the Twitter sphere and social media platforms vibrated with nostalgia on the anniversary of the Arab Uprising on the 25th of January 2020. Take for instance the following Tweet by an anonymous Jordanian literary journalist who has sustained a consistent online presence for 8+ years and had been a neglected disruptive force in the field of literary journalism. He tweets "*we touched the skies…25 January. And found it brimming with shields and meteors… 30 June.*" An interesting finding by Takhteyev and others (2012) was that Twitter was actually making the world local instead of Global. They established that the best indicator of degree of connectivity on Twitter is flight frequency (21). Meaning countries with more flight frequencies to each other will have a more interconnected twitter space. Because flight frequencies are usually highest between neighboring countries, this possibly explains the spillover effect of the Arab uprising. It further establishes that the intertwined Arab Twittersphere wasn't a one-time thing but continues to this day. After the famous attribution of the Arab Spring to social media, a lot has been written about the way social media was used to make the Arab Spring possible. Now, we know that this theory was disproved. But the realization of the potency of social media as an organizing tool propagated the world over. Soon, similar experiences were recorded in other states, where social media was thought to play a major role as an organization and communication tool. Somehow and almost naturally, Twitter was collectively chosen as the platform of choice for state-actors to co-opt civil society and norm entrepreneurs (as will be detailed in the next section). The Twittersphere buzzed with life. This thesis is an

كتابات ديك الجن
@deekblog

وأنّا لمسنا السماء.. ٢٥ يناير
فوجدناها مُلئت حرساً شديداً وشهبا.. ٣٠ يونيو

Translate Tweet
10:29 PM · 25 Jan 21 · Twitter for iPhone

54 Retweets 11 Quote Tweets 734 Likes

Tweet 3 - Arab Spring Anniversary Tweet

exploration of one of the action-patterns within the Arab Twittersphere using a new theoretical framework for understanding Twitter Diplomacy.

The Digital Pilgrimage

In the literature, there seems to be little dispute on who opted the cyberspace first: terrorist organizations and norm entrepreneurs. And it seems in both cases state-actors were either unaware of the content of the messages that cyber space was vibrating with or were under the impression that it was completely inconsequential in the offline world. Yet, it is clear that civil unrest and increasing terrorist recruits forced the sceptics to recalculate the weight assigned to cyber space. For instance, Uysal and Schroeder write that the mere formation of a global civil society highlighted the utility and strength of social media (14). While Pamment (2012) found that the original motivators for MFAs to join social media platforms was to counter extremist narratives and recruitment efforts. The error was detected and rectified by state-actors, and soon the digital pilgrimage began to the cyber mecca. This digital pilgrimage was an intentional and global shift that clearly demonstrates that state-actors exponentially embraced digital platforms. For instance, Obama's administration strongly encouraged federal agencies to adopt 'new media' with the goal of providing information to the American public, communicating with the public and even to offer government services (Bertot, Jaeger and Grimes, 2012). Following the Obama directives, federal agencies migrated en-masse to social media sites such as Facebook and Twitter while also launching websites and blogs through which information could be disseminated and relationships with connected publics could be cultivated (Mergel, 2013). To further facilitate this migration online, the Obama administration issued a series of guidelines and recommendations outlining the risks and benefits of utilizing ‘new media’ in government (Picazo-Vela, Gutiérrez-Martínez and LunaReyes, 2012). According to Snead, the Obama administration’s vision was that of an informed public interacting online with informed policy makers thus increasing the openness and transparency of the government (Snead, 2013; Bjola & Manor, 2018). By 2017, an incomplete list on its website showed that the state department owns more than 800 social media accounts through its missions worldwide on an assortment of platforms (U.S. Department of State, 2017; Shahin & Huang, 2019). Similarly, the data compiled by Twiplomacy[1] clearly illustrates the steady digital pilgrimage by Arab state-actors as below in figure 3, where in 2009 there were only 10 state-actors on the Arabic Twittersphere, which exploded to 125 by 2020. The 10 Arab state-actors who had joined the Twittersphere as early as 2009 are presented in figure 4.

[1] The data used has been obtained from the latest Twiplomacy data sets that has been published on their website. What constitutes as Arab is elaborated on in detail in the methodology section.

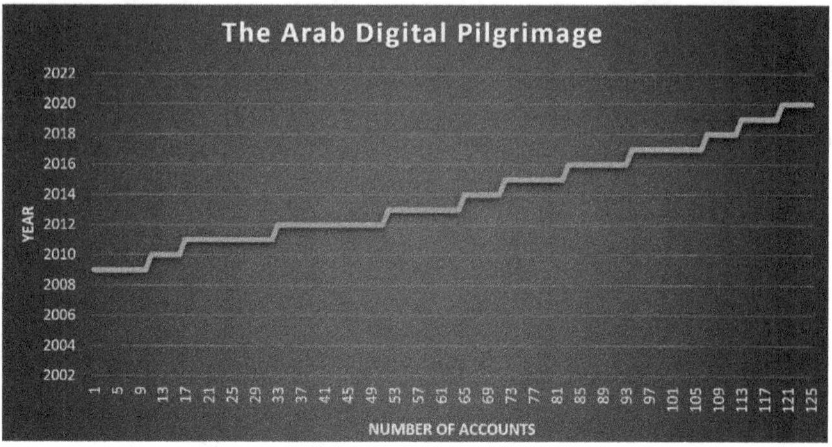

Figure 3 - The Arab Digital Pilgrimage

First state adopters in the Arab Twittersphere

Twitter Handle	Verified Names	Joined Twitter
QueenRania	Rania Al Abdullah	2009
HHShkMohd	HH Sheikh Mohammed	2009
BarhamSalih	Barham Salih	2009
khalidalkhalifa	خالد بن أحمد	2009
MOFAKuwait	وزارة الخارجية	2009
bahdiplomatic	وزارة الخارجية	2009
egyptgovportal	The Egyptian Gov Portal - بوابة الحكومة المصرية	2009
iGABahrain	iGA Bahrain	2009
PalestinePMO	PM of Palestine	2009
Kuwait	دولة الكويت	2009

Table 1 - First state adopters in the Arab Twittersphere

By 2018, 97% of the UN member states were already on Twitter, confirming the undeniable trend (Duncombe, 2018). The digital pilgrims weren't only state-actors, but also encompassed virtually every recognizable IR actor including NGOS and IGOs which had an established a presence on Twitter (18).

Conclusion

Chapter 3 examines the point zero of the emergence of Twitter Diplomacy in the Arab world and argues that it was the Arab blogosphere. It examines how the emergence of the Arab blogosphere was successful at internalizing the norm of gathering information about the government and disseminating it. It then examines briefly the relationship between the Arab Spring and how the Arab Twittersphere emerged and argues that the Arab Twittersphere is a natural heir to the Arab blogosphere. It reinforces this argument by producing evidence of a Tweet by a heavily followed influencer that romanticized the Arab Spring, on its 10-year anniversary. The chapter then argues that the busy Arab Twittersphere, along with the global trend ensured that Twitter is the destination of choice for the Arab digital pilgrimage. Next, chapter 4 will examine theoretical frameworks for Twitter Diplomacy.

Part II:
Proposing

Chapter 4:
A new classification framework for Twitter Diplomacy

Introduction

At last, the narration of the sub-stories that serve as pillars for understanding Twitter Diplomacy are complete. This chapter is the story of Twitter Diplomacy, as a stand-alone story. There has been a steady increment in the research output on the subject that can be categorized as 'Twitter Diplomacy' from different disciplines. Of course, the unknowns remain more than the knowns. This chapter is dedicated to bringing the reader up to date with what we do know, at this point on the topic of Twitter Diplomacy. The chapter then closes with proposing a classification framework for categorizing the different types of Twitter Diplomacy.

Chapter objectives:

4.1 The problem with the existing Twitter Diplomacy theoretical frameworks are:

- A lack of a clear definition of Twitter Diplomacy
- The relatively small literature on Twitter Diplomacy
- The lack of convergence in the literary strands that do examine Twitter Diplomacy

4.2 Furthering a Twitter Diplomacy definition:

- Guided by the definitions furthered by BCW communications firm in their leading reports on Twitter Diplomacy termed Twiplomacy
- Twiplomacy is operationalized instead of Twitter Diplomacy

4.3 Why actors use Twiplomacy:

- Setting the agenda
- Information gathering
- Networking
- Gaining support
- Diaspora engagement
- Crisis communication
- Mobilization

4.4 Actors use Twiplomacy for:

- A horizontal audience
- A vertical audience

4.5 Furthering a new classification system for Twiplomacy:

- Vertical Twiplomacy
    - Internal Vertical Twiplomacy
    - External Vertical Twiplomacy
- Horizontal Twiplomacy
    - Covert Horizontal Twiplomacy
    - Overt Horizontal Twiplomacy

The problem in the existing Twitter Diplomacy theoretical frameworks:

Searching for a definition for Twitter Diplomacy is a daunting task. Not only is there a lack of a theoretical framework for understanding Twitter Diplomacy as an activity, but there isn't enough consensus in its small literature on what Twitter Diplomacy actually is or whether or not it's significant enough to claim a subcategory on its own under Digital Diplomacy. Digital Diplomacy itself is relatively an under studied and possibly under-estimated topic; with a relatively small literature. It has been mainly investigated within three disciplinary lens which almost never relate; public diplomacy, digital diplomacy and diplomatic studies (20). The public diplomacy lens focuses on how digital diplomacy can be used as a tool for diplomatic prestige deficits for a state, how effectively states use digital diplomacy to connect with publics, the reasons for the consistent failure of MFAs of most states to actively engage public online and how digital diplomacy can be used to set the online agendas of the international community (20). The digital diplomacy lens focuses on the use of SNSs to counter online extremist narratives, promote positive national narratives and re-inforce accepted norms and values (20). The diplomatic studies lens focuses on the use of SNSs during geo-political crises, the transition of the diplomatic sphere from clubs to networks that allows the emergence of important nodes within diplomatic networks, the inclusion of more non-state actors within the network and the more public process of diplomacy and diplomats (20). The resultant is a confusing mesh of different concepts with the same terminologies, with the public diplomacy strand almost monopolizing the entire conversation on Twitter Diplomacy, yet only from the perspective of the practice of public diplomacy and completely overlooking its effect on other areas of relevance to IR.

Furthermore, there is a significant number of studies published from an astonishingly wide array of scholarly disciplines that pushes our knowledge of Twitter Diplomacy further, yet does not explicitly mention the term 'Twitter Diplomacy' or any of its close alternatives, and hence is easily bypassed during a first search attempt. This includes literature from social movement research, online social movement research, social network analysis, communication research, protest research, diaspora research, research on the first wave of the Arab Uprisings and many other literary strands. The takeaway is that the rise and pervasiveness of Twitter Diplomacy has had very real epistemological and ontological influences on almost all aspects of human life, translating into the high rate of diffusion into almost every scholarly field.

Furthering a Twitter Diplomacy Definition

To disallow the continuation of the tradition of confusion in the use of terminologies that have similar names but dissimilar definitions, I attempt to operationalize a few definitions guided by the well-executed work of BCW communications firm, the producers of the Twiplomacy project[2]. It's difficult to have any meaningful discussion about Twitter Diplomacy, without at least some reference to Twiplomacy.com. Indeed, one of very few coherent definitions that has some real utility to the action-patterns

[2] Available at www.twiplomacy.com

we see IR actors manifest within Twitter are the terms furthered by BWC communications firm and the way they use them. Even though, even BWC present a few inconsistencies in the use of the term and gather information only on state-actors and hence are naturally implying that state-actors are the only Twitter diplomats, their definitions still demonstrate the most utility and the most neutral tone (or close to it) compared to other definitions proposed so far.

The definition of Twitter Diplomacy is the use of Twitter by an individual or a group of individuals for ideological, social movement, religious, political or humanitarian reasons by influencing audiences through soft power exclusively that will result in favorable results of a political nature in International Relations. The practitioners of Twitter Diplomacy are Twitter Diplomats. I further operationalize that Twitter Diplomats can be state-actors, anti-state actors, transitional state-actors, non-state actors, IGOs, NGOs, activists, religious figure heads, norm entrepreneurs, social movement figure heads and of course terrorist organizations. Using Twitter for posts of a political nature is not sufficient to be considered as Twitter Diplomacy; having an intentional audience and a goal of a political nature in the offline world is necessary. Goals of a political nature are subject to change and evolution in International Relations.

Why actors use Twitter Diplomacy

After extent familiarization with the literature from different literary strands that implicitly reveal information about Twitter Diplomacy that relates to the study of IR, I categorize the use of Twitter Diplomacy for 7 distinct reasons:

- Setting the agenda
- Information gathering
- Networking
- Gaining support
- Diaspora engagement
- Crisis communication
- Mobilization

First, in 2005 (one year before the emergence of Twitter) it was identified that one of the most important uses of digital diplomacy in general is that it provides a new avenue for agenda setting (47). In communication studies, there are two-levels of agenda-setting. First level agenda setting refers to the selection of specific topics to be discussed in outlets that in turn effect which topics are branded as important to the public. This is achieved by repetitive news coverage of certain topics, often with urgency. Second level agenda setting, on the other hand, refers to what associations and perceptions form in the minds of the publics in relation to these topics, or their framing. It is this positive framing of policies to foreign publics that is the ultimate goal of public diplomacy. In the past, these outlets were almost completely monopolized by well-established news outlets. The emergence of new media outlets, however, has provided alternative pathways to agenda-setting including blogs, SNSs and informal agenda-setting through movies and media productions. Agenda-setting through news outlets is considered vertical agenda setting, because of its top-down approach (48). The emergence of SNSs provided a way to bypass the monopoly of large, bureaucratic news organizations that sometimes carry inherent biases against the reporting of specific topics or frames. Agenda-setting through outlets other than news outlets is called horizontal agenda-setting (48). Twitter can serve as both a horizontal and a vertical agenda-setting tool; it could further propagate and enforce the agendas that the news outlets are disseminating or it could allow the reconstruction of the most pressing topics in the publics' agenda. The importance of setting the agenda to policymakers has been captured by studies that showed that policymakers were forced to formulate policies for the issues that were most dominant on national news (48). Furthermore, diplomats use Twitter Diplomacy to set the agenda both with national and foreign publics and also with fellow diplomats. In fact, Twitter Diplomacy allows for the possibility of the reconfiguration in the influence of sidelined states to set the agenda in diplomatic circles. It has been found that the states with the most followers on Twitter are in a unique position to the set the agenda on the global stage and even frame them according to their interests (48). An example of states using Twitter Diplomacy for agenda-setting is the

German MFA's announcement of the Russian expulsion from the G8 during the height of the Crimean crisis and their use of the hashtag #G7 (48), hoping for the hashtag to propagate further and hence gain visibility and importance in the eyes of the public. Similarly, when states were asked by Twiplomacy why they use Twitter, the Israeli MFA tweeted[3] that one of the reasons they use Twitter is to "highlight major issues" in Israel's foreign policy to its global audiences, which corresponds to first and second level agenda setting in the literature. Furthermore, the use of Twitter Diplomacy for agenda-setting and framing has increased in urgency and value since the realization of the fiercely competitive framing environment of Twitter, ready to negatively frame the actions of other actors. This pressures actors to attempt to exert some influence on the framing of events, according to their own interpretations. This leaves actors with only two possible outcomes: frame it or defame it. Second-level agenda setting using framing techniques could similarly be thought of along the lines of Joseph Nye's "whose story wins" argument that he proposes has replaced the historical conclusiveness of "whose army wins" in the moral battle of the states. For instance, when Twiplomacy asked states why they use Twitter, the Estonian MFA tweeted[4] "For us at (@MFAestonia), Twitter is a place to share the Estonian story - highlight our core values, share our deep-rooted convictions and explain our political

---

[3] Available at: https://twitter.com/IsraelMFA/status/1146080360633110529
[4] Available at: https://twitter.com/MFAestonia/status/1144589860298264577

positions […].” This highlights the depth of the conviction of states in the importance of winning the narrative, narrating their story and Twitter’s utility in providing a venue for that. This is especially true since t has been demonstrated that there is no real relationship between the hard power of states and their story’s chance of winning the narrative (49). This means that states that lag behind in hard power have an equal chance of winning the narrative. The importance of attempting to narrate a story that might win is that it creates favorable images of the actor that in the case of states can enhance the brand of the nation (50) . The brand of the nation not only has political and social value, but has substantial economic value as well. Hence, Twitter is an important avenue for promoting an actor’s story through agenda-setting. It is especially important for actors that lack a wide network of outlets for disseminating their story, and for states that lag behind in the global order; because it provides a fighting chance for the lesser heard point of view.

Second, Twitter Diplomacy can be used for information-gathering. Twitter can be a source for gathering information about users that can reveal personal information, ideological inclinations, ethnicity, political opinions and the favorability of policies to the public. This information-gathering capacity is referred to as listening in the public diplomacy literature. Listening to foreign publics is an important part for the adaptive design of favorable public diplomacy policies (15). This is why Switzerland’s public diplomacy efforts used to be organized around listening by using targeted polls (15). Twitter has made listening an easier task; it is now possible to map the public's response to policies and categorize them as positive, negative or neutral (6). Furthermore, twitter listening doesn't just allow Twitter diplomats to design desirable messages to their targeted audiences, but also allows them to better formulate their defenses against their dissenters by listening to their counter-arguments (47). This information-gathering capacity of Twitter wasn't lost on state-actors. For instance, the Director of the Digital communication division at the Polish MFA stated that the Russian and Ukrainian digital accounts were important sources of information for the Polish MFA (20). Similarly, the Lithuanian digital diplomacy unit had a dedicated monitoring division, to keep an eye on other states' online activities (20). The use of Twitter Diplomacy for information-gathering is emerging as a top-priority for states. So much so that recent years has seen an increase in the budget of information-gathering capacities of a lot of MFAs (20). For instance, the digital unit of the British Foreign and Commonwealth office launched a big data analysis unit and an open-source intelligence unit (20), aimed at gathering, analysing and using user data more efficiently. Similarly, the Israeli MFA recruited data scientists for its digital diplomacy unit and the New Zeeland MFA recruited computer scientists for its digital department, also to improve the quantity and quality of information-gathering (20). A noteworthy point is that the more information a node in a network has, the more it becomes central to the entire network (20). This is because networks aggregate around information-sharing nodes, publicly or privately. This serves as an additional motivator for states to develop their information-gathering capacities; to become more central to the international network, as most communication is becoming networked.

Third, Twitter offers an important venue for networking. Social media communication is naturally networked communication. And networks are multi-layered, which makes networked communication also multi-layered. One of the main contributions of SNSs is that they allow for the visualization and analysis of the connections that form at a dyadic level, a triadic level, a clique level, a sub-network level or a network level (6). For instance, it was demonstrated that during the Arab Uprisings, Wael Ghonim had a larger retweet network than Justin Bieber, which allowed for the electrifying propagation of his messages (51). Justin Bieber – an American singer – had more followers than Wael Ghonim at that time by a factor of 100. Yet, Bieber had a large number of passive listeners and a low level of connectivity and trust between his followers, also known as a 'clustering coefficient' (51). The large-scale follower participation in issues of interest is what allows social relationships to emerge between participants and the formation of what is called participant-issue network. Sophisticated machine-aided mapping of networks guided by social network analysis allow Twitter diplomats to identify important nodes in a network, understand the nature of the network, and readjust their communication strategies on Twitter to make the most use of networks of interest. Another example for the utilization of Twitter Diplomacy for networking that was mapped by the use of computer-assisted mapping is the deduction of only 27 meaningful nodes on 1% of the Egyptian Twittersphere during the first wave of the Arab Uprisings, whose networking efforts were so potent that they dominated a large segment of the Egyptian Twittersphere (51). Furthermore, Twitter diplomats use Twitter Diplomacy to find an entrance point to new networks, maintain their position within an established network or renegotiate their position within it. For instance, Cassidy and Manor showed that one of the most important reasons for the migration of most MFAs online is to be able to follow their peers (20), and hence enter a network they are already a part of. For instance, the Icelandic Foreign Ministry is the most well-connected foreign ministry in the world currently, with 147 mutual peer connections (52), while the Lithuanian MFA[5] tweeted that "Twitter is a gateway into a bigger network where different levels of diplomacy can be explained or illustrated in just 280 characters, a short video clip or an infographic," when asked why they use Twitter Diplomacy. It is seemingly an easy task to find an entrance point to a new network on SNSs because of the well-documented tendency of SNSs to aid the aggregation of users with similarities to maintain homophily. And eventually echo-chambers. Of course,

---

[5] Available at: https://twitter.com/LithuaniaMFA/status/1144605889493684224

similarities within this context could mean anything that the user choses to identify with that can encompass nationality, ethnicity, gender, religion, social class, location, political ideology or a specific interest that guides self-identity. Hence, Twitter diplomats often use Twitter Diplomacy to engage in networking activities with counter-parts and the public, simultaneously.

Fourth, according to the literature that the ultimate goal of digital diplomacy is to secure the support of the public (20). This could be domestic or foreign public support. In 2018, Bjola and Manor proposed the concept of Domestic Digital Diplomacy (DDD), which they defined as the use of SNSs by a government to build domestic support for its foreign policies. They explained how the Obama administration's dedicated Twitter handle (@TheIranDeal) is a fitting example of DDD; as its goal was to secure the support of the American public and its congress for the Iran deal. However, DDD is limiting in its scope, because it assumes that the only issues states use Twitter to raise support for are foreign policies. On the contrary, actors including states take to Twitter to develop support for their internal state issues as well. This can include raising support for specific policies through public awareness campaigns or raising support for electoral candidates. For instance, Twitter is a very important venue during election times that multiple states' Twitterspheres were reported to have increased activity shortly before elections including Italy, Bosnia, Herzegovina and Sweden. New public diplomacy, on the other hand, is the use of digital platforms to secure the support of foreign publics for foreign policies. For example, in 2012, Metzgar examined the US State Department's virtual embassy to Iran and found that the embassy's online activities enabled it to manage America's offline image and increase American offline soft power resources among the Iranian population (20); thus, increasing the chances of support for American policies by Iranian publics. Similarly, one of the top priorities for the Government of Malta's Twitter Diplomacy communication strategies seems to be to "raise public awareness" of government efforts.[6]

Fifth, Twitter Diplomacy can be used for critical communication during times of crisis. For instance, in September 2013, Westgate Mall in Nairobi, Kenya was the target of a terror attack. Al Shabab, a U.S designated terrorist group besieged Westgate Mall for 4 days and resulted in 67 deaths and 175 wounded victims (19). During the siege, Kenyan state-actors such as the Kenyan police and the Kenyan Interior Ministry overwhelmingly took to Twitter to update each other and the Nairobi public on events on the ground, instructions and advice for the safety of the citizens (19). Interestingly, the use of Twitter for critical communication during a time of crises wasn't just an unusual first impulse of Kenyan state-actors alone, but appeared to be the unanimous first impulse of all responding parties. This includes Al Shabab, who

[6] Available at: https://twitter.com/MaltaGov/status/1145980135805542400

announced their responsibility for the terror attack, also on Twitter. Another ready example for the growing importance of Twitter as a critical communication tool during times of crises are the global responses by almost all actors during the Covid-19 pandemic. For instance, the first state-actor to use Twitter to communicate about the emerging crises that was about to bring the world to a halt in a few months was Philippine's foreign minister Teddy Locisn Jr who tweeted on January 19 2020, "DOH (Department of Health) is on top of this along with Airport authorities to screen new arrivals from China. Last thing we can handle is this kind of epidemic [. . .]"[7] (52). Similarly, on the 15th January 2020, the Indonesian government took to Twitter to announce the installation of thermo-scanners at 135 entrance points to the country[8] (52). UK Prime Minister Boris Johnson announced his infection with Covid-19 with a tweet[9], while France invested in promoting the hashtag #JeResteChezMoi (I stay at home) to communicate to the French public the importance of staying at home (52). The Covid-19 pandemic not only catalysed the already growing trend of Twitter Diplomacy for political communication, but also visually highlighted the extent of the acceptability of new actors in IR. For instance, the WHO is officially the most followed IGO on Twitter with 9.4 million followers, as of June 2021. The WHO was quick to utilize Twitter for sharing

---

[7] Available at: https://twitter.com/teddyboylocsin/status/1218732893897293824
[8] Available at: https://twitter.com/setkabgoid/status/1219940114547130368
[9] Available at: https://twitter.com/BorisJohnson/status/1243496858095411200

updates, instructions and educational material to its followers. The WHO didn't just use Twitter Diplomacy for crisis communication, but it also did it very effectively by designing engaging digital campaigns, challenges and introducing hashtags. For instance, the WHO launched the #SafeHands challenge to promote the power of clean hands against the covid-19 virus, which became a global digital trend[10] (53). Similarly, Dr Tedros Adnahom's personal Twitter handle exploded from 2,200 followers in early 2020 to 1.4 million follower, as of June 2021. One of the most telling steps adopted by the WHO during a testing time of global crises was the hiring of 4 new staff for managing their digital platforms to the already existing team of 2. This reveals the WHO's understanding of the efficacy of Twitter Diplomacy for communication during times of crises. Another example for a newly emerging actor in IR that used the covid-19 crisis to negotiate a more active role in global IR is Twitter itself. Twitter, as an MNC, used Twitter Diplomacy as a crisis communication tool to renegotiate the spectrum of its acceptable role in IR. Consider Twitter's active role in disallowing the propagation of disinformation about the coronavirus. Twitter engaged in an extensive and urgent verification campaign of health experts across the world, including health experts from IGOs and state-sanctioned health experts such as Health ministers (53). The health expert verification campaign was expanded to a general

[10] Available at: https://twitter.com/WHO/status/1238404251933704193

verification campaign of foreign ministry accounts, leaders of states and Twitter influencers. After verification campaigns, Twitter engaged in assertive suspension campaigns that world leaders weren't immune to. For instance, one of the suspended accounts for spreading misinformation about the novel coronavirus was the presidential account of Nicholas Madura (@PresidencialVen). In March 2020, Twitter also suspended the account of Venezuela's Vice President Delcy Rodríguez (@DrodriguezVen) for 'unusual activity.' Twitter also flagged content that wasn't necessarily misinformation but was at least misrepresentation for political interests. The most visible example of Twitter either deliberately or accidentally using the crisis to grow its ability to sway political narratives is the assertive flagging of the Chinese-American Twitter war about the origins of the virus. Twitter flagged Tweets that misrepresented information about the origins of the virus by adding a Twitter generated message that said "Get the facts about the COVID-19," and thus disallowing the historical tendencies of states to engage in propagandas for political gains.

Sixth, Twitter Diplomacy can used as a re-engagement tool with diasporic communities. Indeed, a large body of scholars have established that digital platforms have been increasingly deployed to connect with diasporic communities. For example, the Israeli embassy ran a campaign called #IsraelRetweetedMe to engage the Jewish diaspora where it allowed user generated content to be re-shared on its page (17). Hence, it used Twitter Diplomacy to re-engage with the Jewish diaspora and strengthen their bonds with the state of Israel. This can result in plenty of positive outcomes for the state of Israel, including increasing the chance of support by engaged diasporic communities to support foreign policies in their current state of citizenship that are favorable to the state of Israel. Similarly, Twitter Diplomacy can be used *by* diasporic communities. For instance, it was the Ethiopian diaspora community in the U.S that was responsible for sparking off the large-scale anti-government protests in Ethiopia. Similarly, when Twiplomacy asked why state-actors used Twitter, the Armenian MFA listed "[…] contact with the Armenian community in all the corners of the world"[11] as one of its reasons for using Twitter Diplomacy. The on-going Palestinian save sheikh jarrah movement is another example of a very distinct two-way utilization of Twitter Diplomacy of citizen journalists and norm entrepreneurs within Palestine directed at Palestinian diasporic communities scattered around the world and later *by* it.

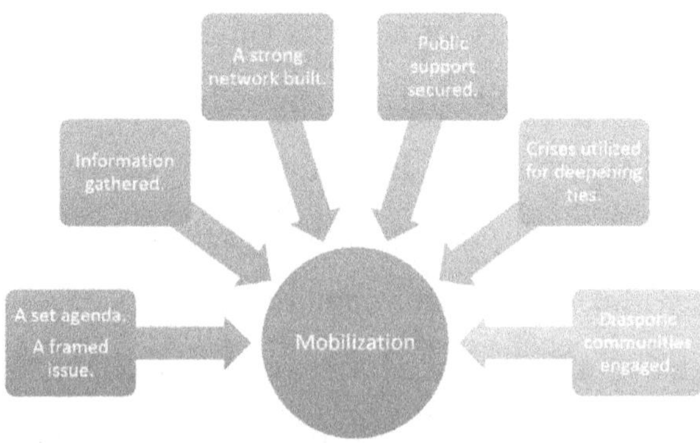

[11] Available at: https://twitter.com/MFAofArmenia/status/1153354323520303105

Seventh, is the use of Twitter Diplomacy for mobilization. A heavily contested role by some. A heavily cited role by others. Yet, weather real or perceived, Twitter plays *some* role in catalyzing large-scale mobilizations. Or maybe all it does is visualize *how* mobilization happens. So, there's two ways to think of Twitter and mobilization; Twitter may be seen as an enzyme that catalyzes the equation that leads to large-scale people mobilization, or it can be seen as a coloring agent that simply allows us to see the chemical equation. In this case, the coloring agent is social network analysis. An interesting question to ask at this point would be: is Mobilization through Twitter Diplomacy achieved only as a *result* of the successful use of Twitter for the 6 Twitter Diplomacy uses listed above? In other words, are mobilizations which have some form of relationship with Twitter only achieved after successfully setting the agenda, framing the issue, gathering enough supporter and dissenter information, establishing a participative network with high levels of trust, gaining substantial levels of public support, maintaining communication during times of crises and engaging a support base that transcends one given geographical area? The question of my current investigation. Yet what is apparent now is the incessant causality that state actors often associate with Twitter when any type of mobilization happens. For instance, in the leaked voice record between Prince Hamzah Bin Hussein and the man who identified himself as the head of the army after the alleged coup attempt in Jordan, the man explicitly asks Prince Hamzah to 'cease his tweeting activities' (1). To have one of the major demands from an actor who is perceived to be compromising the stability of the state be 'stop tweeting' is a testimony to the actual or perceived potency of the Twittersphere in shaping political discourse within states. Similarly, the perceived threat of Twitter as a tool for mobilization by the Ethiopian diasporic community was so grave that it led the Ethiopian government to install a 6-month state of emergency and blocked both Twitter and Facebook (28).

Who actors use Twitter Diplomacy for

It seems that specific action-patterns are being practiced within the Twittersphere. Because of the large scale participation of actors and individuals with social media in general and Twitter in specific, these action-patterns have become an unconscious knowledge that we haven't articulated properly but have acted out masterfully. This why a close investigation of the Twittersphere and its literature produces observations on how Twitter Diplomacy is being practiced. The observations on who actors use Twitter Diplomacy for are the basis for the theoretical categorization that will be outlined in the next section. Twiplomats use Twitter Diplomacy in two distinct ways; for horizontal communication and for vertical communication.

Horizontally

Actors are using Twitter Diplomacy to communicate with counter-parts, as outlined in the 3rd use of Twitter Diplomacy in the section above. The concept of networked diplomacy was furthered by (Clarke, 2015; Slaughter, 2009; Zaharna, Arsenault and Fisher, 2013) and has been defined as the practice of engaging in political and social discussions with various actors on multiple platforms (48). These various actors are generally understood as other states, IGOs, INGOs, private individuals and global civil society. I make the further argument that it even includes communicating with terrorist organizations and believe further research should be conducted on this topic. As early as 2009, Anne-Marie Slaughter has outlined how diplomacy has become interconnected, networked and global, amongst other scholars (48). Similarly, one of the most interesting arguments that some scholars have also made is that social media networks provide the same opportunity for sidelined states to re-negotiate global standing as do multilateral institutions like the UN (48). One of the important reasons for this new-found opportunity to re-negotiate the global pecking order is that the new formed cyber-network doesn't automatically mirror real-life diplomatic influence of states on the global scene (Slaughter, 2009). According to (48) an actor can establish influence on the network by becoming a 'super-node' within the network; a super-connected, central node to the entire network. States with more online following do exert higher influence on shaping the global narrative, setting the global agenda and 'winning the story' (Beckfield, 2003). One of the most interesting opportunities that this new networked diplomacy has provided is the chance for direct and public communication between state-actors, without resorting to their respective embassies or MFAs. And indeed, the opportunity has been identified and utilized very well by state-actors. In fact, it seems that state-actors who aren't on the MFA or the embassies' pay-roll (e.g.: heads of states) have been tremendously more successful than embassies or MFAs, in virtually all states. This could be attributed to research that found that MFAs were very change-resistant and in favor of information-keeping (Copeland 2013, McNutt 2014). The final outcome was that Twitter Diplomacy main uses was to engage horizontally with other actors on the world stage. For instance, when Saudi human rights activists Rahaf and Samar Al Badawi were arrested, Canada's Global Affair Minister and the Canadian MFA took to twitter to call on Saudi officials to release them (19). Saudi Arabia reacted to the tweet by recalling its ambassador, expelling the Canadian ambassador and suspending a few economic and investment ties (19). Furthermore, the Saudi MFA tweeted back to the Canadian MFA that "*the Canadian position is an overt and blatant interference in the internal affairs of the Kingdom of #SaudiArabia and is in contravention of the most basic international norms and all the charters governing relations between States*" (19). The Twitter spat was apparently so visible that it inspired a pro-government Twitter handle to tweet an image of an Air Canada flight in the Toronto skyline with text inserted into the image that read: "*sticking one's nose where it doesn't belong!*" and a caption that read "*He who interferes with what doesn't concern him finds what doesn't please him*" (19). This tweet went viral. Not only did it go viral, but it is widely thought that this twitter exchange was one of the major factors to the continued trade freeze between the two countries, as anger erupted over the tweet that was understood as a direct link September 11 (19). Similarly, Narendra Modi's Twitter Diplomacy practice of sharing selfies with world-leaders during an official state-visit was so noticeable by his followers that the lack of a selfie with Canadian Prime Minister Justin Trudeau was interpreted as a diplomatic insult to the Canadian Prime Minister to signify irritation over the Canadian support and asylum offered to Indian Sikh separatists (19). A further example of horizontal Twitter Diplomacy efforts is Dr. Anwar Gargash's masterful diplomatic message[12] to Bahrain:

Tweet 4 - Anwar Gargash's diplomatic message to Bahrain

[12] Translation: We know, and trust, that the brotherly Bahrain is the first that respects and takes into account the rights of its neighbors,
And that the Manama, in its legacy is the master of customs in the appropriate and wise interaction,
And doesn't accept that violations, whatever they are, are from her side.
The Bahrain laid down its customs and its leadership kept it alive, and hence earned the respect and trust of its neighbours.

Vertically

As established in *the uses of Twitter Diplomacy*, other than to engage, network and communicate with counter-parts, Twitter Diplomacy is used to communicate with the public. A longitudinal observation of the Twittersphere, the action-patterns within it, and the literature it has so far seem to clearly signify the use of Twitter Diplomacy for both communicating 'domestically' and communicating with foreign publics (public diplomacy). An example of using Twitter Diplomacy for the benefit of a local or domestic audience is Barack Obama's Tweet during the recent American Presidential elections to Georgia voters:

> **Barack Obama**
> @BarackObama
>
> Georgia voters—If you're in line before the polls close at 7 pm, stay there. You have the right to vote, no matter how long it takes. If you have questions, call the Georgia voter protection hotline at 1-888-730-5816. Let's bring this home.
>
> 2:35 AM · Jan 6, 2021 · Twitter Web App
>
> **34.8K** Retweets **1,096** Quote Tweets **328.5K** Likes

Tweet 5- Barack Obama's message to domestic public

A further example of Twitter Diplomacy for local or domestic audiences is King Salman's tweet[13] to the Saudi public:

[13] Translation:

سلمان بن عبدالعزيز
@KingSalman
المملكة العربية السعودية حساب حكومي رسمي

أيها الشعب الكريم : تستحقون أكثر ومهما فعلت لن أوفيكم حقكم، أسأل الله على أن يعينني وإياكم على خدمة الدين والوطن، ولاتنسوني من دعائكم.

Translate Tweet

1:21 AM · Jan 30, 2015 · Twitter for iPhone

369.3K Retweets 1,592 Quote Tweets 139.7K Likes

Tweet 6 – King Salman's Tweet to the Saudi Citizens

On the other hand, an example on using Twitter Diplomacy for communicating with a foreign public (or public diplomacy) is seen in Iranian Imam Khamenei's Tweet[14] to all Arabic speaking publics, in his Arabic Twitter handle:

الإمام الخامنئي
@ar_khamenei

إنّها بداية عصر ما بعد أمريكا.

Translate Tweet

11:38 PM · Feb 7, 2021 · Twitter Web App

4,695 Retweets 705 Quote Tweets 18.2K Likes

Tweet 7 - Imam Khamenei's Tweet to Arab audiences

Kind people: you deserve more and whatever I do I can't do you justice, I ask God to assist me and you in serving our religion and nation, and don't forget me from your prayers.

[14] Translation:
It's the beginning of a Post-American era.

Proposing a new classification system for Twitter Diplomacy

Following the arguments laid in the sections above, this thesis proposes the following framework for classifying Tweets. Tweets can be categorized to two categories depending on the audience: *Vertical Twitter Diplomacy (V.T)* and *Horizontal Twitter Diplomacy (H.T)*. Vertical Twitter Diplomacy has two main categories: *Internal Vertical Twitter Diplomacy (I.V.T)* and *External Vertical Twitter Diplomacy (E.V.T)*.

A Classification framework for Twitter Diplomacy

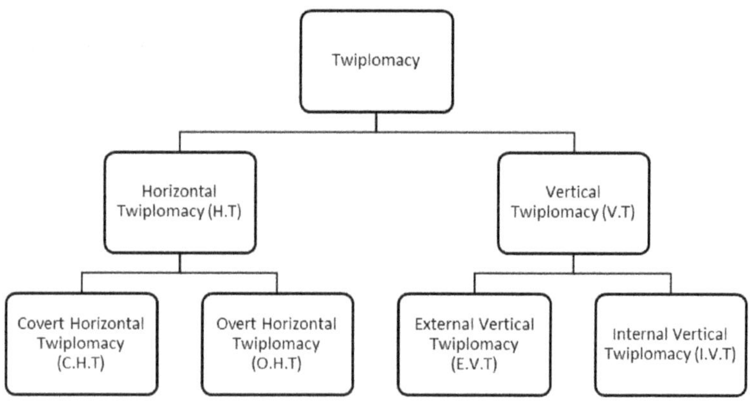

Figure 4 – Classification framework for Twitter Diplomacy

Horizontal Twitter Diplomacy refers to Twitter Diplomacy where the main audience is another Twiplomat. While Vertical Twitter Diplomacy refers to Twitter Diplomacy where the main audience is the public.

Horizontal Twitter Diplomacy is further divided into two categories: overt and covert. Overt Horizontal Twitter Diplomacy

(O.H.T) is made public, even though the main audience is the intended Twiplomat. These include 'tagging' a Twiplomat in tweets, 'liking' the counterpart's tweets, 'retweeting' their tweets, 'replying' to their tweets and following them. Usually, overt Horizontal Twitter Diplomacy is publicized because the interactions are of consequence in IR. While Covert Horizontal Twitter Diplomacy is not public and hence has only one audience; the other Twitter Diplomat. This involves the use of Direct Messaging and blocking.

Types of Horizontal Twitter Diplomacy

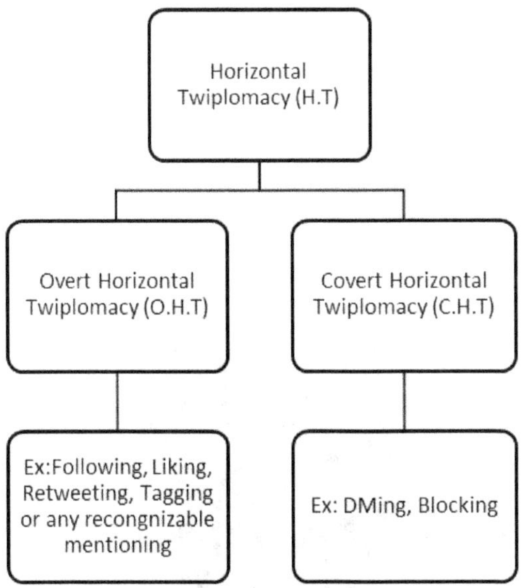

Figure 5- Types of Horizontal Twitter Diplomacy

An example of an OHT is the following, where Abdallah Bin Zayed shares an image of a fellow Twiplomat with a message wishing him well.

Tweet 8 - OHT example

Another example of an OHT is Barack Obama's Tweet:

Tweet 9- OHT example 2

Vertical Twitter Diplomacy is further divided on two categories depending on the audience: internal and external. Internal Vertical Twitter Diplomacy refers to the practice of Twitter Diplomacy to a public that shares the same identification as the Twiplomat. The identification could be a nationality, an ethnicity, a gender, a social cause, a movement, an ideology, a religion or a political goal. For example, for state-actors Internal Vertical Twitter Diplomacy involves influencing and communicating to their internal (i.e.: domestic) publics, while for a social movement figurehead internal vertical Twitter Diplomacy involves influencing and communicating to internal supporters of the social movement, and for terrorist figureheads internal vertical Twitter Diplomacy is influencing and communicating to their internal pool of supporters. On the other hand, external vertical Twitter Diplomacy refers to the practice of Twitter Diplomacy to a public that doesn't share the same identification as the Twiplomat. For a state-actor external vertical Twitter Diplomacy involves influencing and communicating to external (i.e., foreign publics), to social movement figureheads external vertical Twitter Diplomacy involves influencing and communicating to external publics that don't support the social movement, and for terrorist figureheads external vertical Twitter Diplomacy is influencing and communicating to publics outside of the pool of active supporters. Ideally, the goal is to construct a bridge to allow for communication.

The point of reference should be specified by the researcher because a Twiplomat will always have more than one identifying feature. For example, a state-actor Twiplomat could also be a religious figurehead and a social movement head. Hence 'internal vertical Twitter Diplomacy' with religion as a reference point will include all members of that specific religion. While an IVT, with the state as a reference point will only include the Twiplomat's fellow citizens.

An example of an EVT (while taking the state as the fixed reference point) is Mohamed Bin Rashid's message to 'the Arab youth.'

HH Sheikh Mohammed
@HHShkMohd
الإمارات العربية المتحدة حساب حكومي رسمي

For the 8th year, the Arab youth finds the UAE the best place to work & live in, followed by Canada, the US and Britain. My message to them is the UAE was & will always be your country, a part of a beautiful Arab world that will continue prospering with your energy & aspirations.

11:33 AM · Apr 30, 2019 · Twitter for iPhone

398 Retweets 18 Quote Tweets 1,605 Likes

Tweet 10 – EVT example

On the other hand, an example of IVT is King Salman's Tweet[15] to Saudi citizens on the Saudi national day:

---

[15] Translation:
In the memory of the national day, we take pride in a great nation, in faithful nationals, and we thank god for grating us safety and stability and nationalism, which you're

سلمان بن عبدالعزيز
@KingSalman
المملكة العربية السعودية حساب حكومي رسمي

في ذكرى اليوم الوطني نفتخر بوطنٍ عظيم، ومواطنين أوفياء،
ونحمد الله على ما منّ به علينا من أمنٍ واستقرارٍ ولُحمةٍ
وطنية، كان لكم ولآبائكم من قبلكم دوراً كبيراً في ترسيخها،
متطلعين لمستقبلٍ أجمل بسواعد أبنائنا وبناتنا.
حفظ الله وطننا من كل مكروه.

Translate Tweet

10:00 PM · Sep 23, 2020 · Twitter for iPhone

223.1K Retweets **4,348** Quote Tweets **258.2K** Likes

Tweet 11 - EVT example 2

It is important to remember that Tweets can have more than one audience and Tweets seldom fall into only one categorically. For instance, consider the following examples:

HH Sheikh Mohammed
@HHShkMohd
الإمارات العربية المتحدة حساب حكومي رسمي

Congratulations @narendramodi and the people of India upon your election win. We look forward to advancing our strategic bilateral relations further and working together for the progress and prosperity of our people.

3:44 PM · May 24, 2019 · Twitter for iPhone

1,264 Retweets **62** Quote Tweets **6,314** Likes

Tweet 12 - Example of Tweet with multiple classifications

---

before you your fathers played a big role in anchoring, looking to a future that is more beautiful through the forearms of our sons and daughters.
May God protect our nation from every harm.

The Tweet can clearly be classified as speaking to both a Twiplomatic counterpart and a foreign public. Yet, the degree with which the Tweet falls into either category is what will allow the Tweet to be classified primarily into one of the classifications.

Part III:
Testing

Chapter 5:

Who do Arab state-actors Tweet for? – The what and the how.

Introduction

This Chapter outlines the specific question that guided this entire project. It establishes what the preliminary expectations are and proceeds to outline the methodology. The methodology attempts to outline the steps that guided the researcher to the highest degree possible without alienating the interdisciplinary reader. There remains a segment of the data manipulation that have been omitted from the book and will be provided upon request to fellow researchers.

Chapter objectives:

5.1 The What – outlining the research question:

5.2 The How – Methodology:

- Identifying trends in the Arab Twittersphere
- Extracting the samples for the selected
- Developing the Parameters

The What – the Research Question

To specify the purpose of this investigative study, I ask a precise and specific question: Who are the main audiences of selected Arab state-actors on Twitter, guided by the proposed theoretical categorization framework that was developed in part 2? The justification for choosing the question is three fold: a) to test the new theoretical framework, b) to explore the Arabic Twittersphere which is virtually unexplored and c) to identify any specific action-patterns in the region that arguably made Twitter Diplomacy what it is today. The expectations from this exploration are that most Arab-state actors would be predominantly engaged in Internal Vertical Twitter Diplomacy policies (IVT), as opposed to trying to perform public diplomacy efforts (External Vertical Twitter Diplomacy or EVT) or Horizontal Twitter Diplomacy (HT). The justification for this expectation is the persistence of the post-Arab-spring Arab world order, which is simmering in chaos that is further compounded by the ongoing Covid-19 pandemic, the Beirut Port Explosion, geopolitical tensions, and a very unusual Palestinian movement that may or may not last. It is expected that in circumstances where state-leaders' around the world are being challenged by their people on their covid-19 responses in general, the Arab states in specific will be more challenged because of the local circumstances of the region.

RQ: Using the proposed categorization framework, who are the main audiences of the selected Arab state-actors' Twitter Diplomacy efforts?

H: The proposed theoretical framework is a useful tool in identifying the main audience of the selected Arab state actors' Twitter Diplomacy efforts.

E: The selected Arab state-actors' Twitter Diplomacy efforts are mostly IVT.

The How - Methodology

Identifying trends in the Arab Twittersphere using secondary data analysis to guide selection of the accounts to be chosen as case-studies:

The first step that was employed in trying to answer the raised research question was a review of the Twitter data sets made available by the Twiplomacy website. The latest Twiplomacy Twitter data sets were published in July 2020 and are available for download at the end of the study (54). The purpose of exploring secondary data sets was guided by the knowledge of the lack of attention the Arab Twittersphere received by researchers in general and the gap in the literature (and the mainstream news) of any trends within the Arab Twittersphere. To extract the relevant information, the data sets were manipulated in 3 phases. In phase 1, all Arabic language accounts were filtered. The Twiplomacy data sets includes a column with the detected language of the Twitter handle. There were three limitations to phase 1; inaccuracies in language detection, undetermined languages and the use of 'ar' for both Arabic and Armenian. Hence, the findings' accuracy was vulnerable to the language detection limitations of the original Twiplomacy data set.

This called for the need for Phase 2. In phase 2, all accounts based within Arab states were filtered. This is made possible by the location column that Twiplomacy's researchers made available. Here, Arab states were operationalized as: Algeria, Bahrain, Comoros, Djibouti, Egypt, Iraq, Jordan, Kuwait, Lebanon, Libya, Mauritania, Morocco, Oman, Palestine, Qatar, Saudi Arabia, Somalia, Sudan, Syria, Tunisia, United Arab Emirates and Yemen. Yet, the problem with Phase 2 is that it leaves out accounts relevant to the Arab Twittersphere that aren't based physically in the operationalized 22 Arab states. This is why I saw the need for a final Phase 3. In Phase 3, the full Twiplomacy data set containing (n=1,089) was manually reviewed in search for accounts that are relevant to the Arab Twittersphere. This was mainly done through detection of names that have relevance to the Arabic language, according to the judgment of the researcher. For instance, the Twitter handle of the Iraq embassy (@Iembassy) did not fulfil neither the language filter, which was detected as English not Arabic, nor the location filter, which was also undetected. Similarly, the account handle of the Yemeni MOFA (@yemen_mofa) was undetermined on both location and language. Hence, both of these accounts would have been completely bypassed if only Phases 1 and 2 were employed.

The resulting accounts were (n=131). Yet, after further dropping suspended and deleted accounts (n=6), the resulting verified state-accounts on the Arab Twittersphere were (n=125).

Suspended and deleted accounts were identified by manually validating the active Twitter presence of each Twitter handle.

The results were the visual identification of unmapped trends within the Arab Twittersphhere, which will be presented in Chapter 6. The familiarization with the Arab Twittersphere, combined with the results of the trend-extraction guided the researcher to select the 4 Twitter Diplomats that will serve as case-studies in this project. The selected Twitter Diplomats were: King Salman, Mohamed Bin Rashid, Abdallah Bin Zayed and Adel Al Jubeir.

Mohamed Bin Rashid ranks as the second most followed state-actor in the Arab Twittersphere, closely behind Queen Rania Al Abdallah of Jordan. Similarly, King Salman ranks as the third most followed state-actor within the Arab Twittersphere and Abdallah Bin Zayed as the fourth. Queen Rania is an important state-sanctioned actor and her consistent emergence as the most followed state-actor on the Arab Twittersphere is in itself a phenomenon worth investigating, yet she does not play as active a role as state-leaders in either the Arab geopolitics or foreign policies. Even though, she does so on cyberspace. Hence, for the purposes of attempting to design a meaningful study that provides trends true of state-actors and not cosmetic state-actors, Queen Rania was not selected. This naturally allowed for the selection of Mohamed Bin Rashid, who in recent years has harnessed a more prominent role in Arab geopolitics, King Salman, who naturally sits in a unique position in Arabian geopolitics and Abdallah Bin Zayed, simply by deciding to study those who have succeeded in securing the biggest audiences. For the fourth case study, a gap in the data sets of Twiplomacy was captured; it lacked quite a lot of Arab state-actors. This includes the account of Adel Al Jubeir, the Saudi Foreign Minister. If Adel Al Jubeir was a part of the original data set, he would have ranked as the 7th most followed state-actor on the Arab Twittersphere and the 2nd most followed Saudi state-actor. To allow for the identification of possible patterns within states, 2 Saudi accounts and 2 Emirati accounts were selected. This, along with the prominence of the selected state-actors in Arabian geopolitics and the geopolitical rise of both K.S.A and the U.A.E were thought optimal to provide a testing ground for the classification framework developed earlier.

Extracting the samples for the selected 4 case-studies:

Now that the selected Twitter handles have been selected, a sample of Tweets is required for each of the Twitter Diplomats. Twitter automatically archives Tweets after a certain limit. This means they have to be manually extracted. The timeline for which the tweets will be extracted is specified as 01-01-2015 till 13-04-2021 for all the accounts. The Tweets have been extracted through Jupytor notebook – a server-client application that allows you to run your notebook from a browser. The language used was Python. To launch the Jupyter dashboard, the code I wrote below is standard practice on the command prompt:

```
C:\Users\noor.suwwan>noorEnv\Scripts\activate

(noorEnv) C:\Users\noor.suwwan>jupyter notebook
[I 12:11:25.363 NotebookApp] Serving notebooks from local directory: C:\Users\noor.suwwan
[I 12:11:25.363 NotebookApp] Jupyter Notebook 6.2.0 is running at:
[I 12:11:25.378 NotebookApp] http://localhost:8888/?token=1c0d7afc2f723d9926ebaf43651f25d4dd9de3080fb24a02
[I 12:11:25.378 NotebookApp]  or http://127.0.0.1:8888/?token=1c0d7afc2f723d9926ebaf43651f25d4dd9de3080fb24a02
[I 12:11:25.378 NotebookApp] Use Control-C to stop this server and shut down all kernels (twice to skip confirmation).
[C 12:11:25.628 NotebookApp]

    To access the notebook, open this file in a browser:
        file:///C:/Users/noor.suwwan/AppData/Roaming/jupyter/runtime/nbserver-12916-open.html
    Or copy and paste one of these URLs:
        http://localhost:8888/?token=1c0d7afc2f723d9926ebaf43651f25d4dd9de3080fb24a02
     or http://127.0.0.1:8888/?token=1c0d7afc2f723d9926ebaf43651f25d4dd9de3080fb24a02
[I 12:11:41.327 NotebookApp] 302 GET /?token=1c0d7afc2f723d9926ebaf43651f25d4dd9de3080fb24a02 (::1) 3.000000ms
[W 12:12:16.975 NotebookApp] Notebook noorEnv/TwitterArchiveforNoor.ipynb is not trusted
[I 12:12:19.509 NotebookApp] Kernel started: f8e4c8d5-07a8-4e9e-97b5-ef83d7c12b27, name: python3
[I 12:12:41.659 NotebookApp] Kernel started: 2f372c2f-b0fc-4acc-ac8d-881a60eceebb, name: python3
[I 12:14:42.274 NotebookApp] Saving file at /noorEnv/TwitterFollowListforNoor.ipynb
```

Code 1 - Command prompt window that launches the Jupyter notebook

The following are the specific codes I used for extracting the tweets:

Mohammed Bin Rashid (@HHShkMohd)

```
import snscrape.modules.twitter as sntwitter     #snscrape is a Python library that bypasses Twitter's API to get as many or all tweets from a user. It is essentially a webscraper
import pandas as pd                               #pandas is a Python library used for data analysis and manipulation

# Environment--------
#must have Python 3.8 on your laptop
#pip install pandas tweepy
#snscrape from github link.. as in, pip install git+https://snscrape.git
#replace the 'from:' field with wanted users and dates next to it
#for more information on what kind of data to get using snscrape, search "snscrape modules"

# Creating list to append tweet data to
tweets_list1 = []

# Using TwitterSearchScraper to scrape data and append tweets to list
# Here we loop thorugh the searchScraper module to get the retrieved tweets and append them to a list
#we try to get as much information as possible, including the tweet's date, language, replies, likes, retweeets, device source, and the tweet ID
#We have the since: and until: options to specify the dates we want, which is dependent on when the specific user started tweeting or when they joined Twitter..
for i,tweet in enumerate(sntwitter.TwitterSearchScraper('from:HHShkMohd since:2015-01-01 until:2021-03-14').get_items()):
    tweets_list1.append([tweet.date, tweet.id, tweet.content, tweet.user.username, tweet.lang, tweet.replyCount, tweet.retweetCount, tweet.likeCount, tweet.source, tweet.url])

# Creating a dataframe from the tweets list above
tweets_df1 = pd.DataFrame(tweets_list1, columns=['Datetime', 'Tweet Id', 'Text', 'Username', 'Language', 'Replies', 'Retweets','Likes', 'Device','Link'])


print(tweets_df1)
#Converting the data frame into an Excel sheet
tweets_df1.to_csv('C:/Users/ausit/twitterData/HHShkMohd.csv', encoding='utf-8-sig', index = True)
```

Code 2 - Mohmed Bin Rashid

Adel Al Jubeir (@AdelAljubeir)

```
import snscrape.modules.twitter as sntwitter     #snscrape is a Python library that bypasses Twitter's API to get as many or all tweets from a user. It is essentially a webscraper
import pandas as pd                               #pandas is a Python library used for data analysis and manipulation

# Environment--------
#must have Python 3.8 on your laptop
#pip install pandas tweepy
#snscrape from github link.. as in, pip install git+https://snscrape.git
#replace the 'from:' field with wanted users and dates next to it
#for more information on what kind of data to get using snscrape, search "snscrape modules"

# Creating list to append tweet data to
tweets_list1 = []

# Using TwitterSearchScraper to scrape data and append tweets to list
# Here we loop thorugh the searchScraper module to get the retrieved tweets and append them to a list
#we try to get as much information as possible, including the tweet's date, language, replies, likes, retweeets, device source, and the tweet ID
#We have the since: and until: options to specify the dates we want, which is dependent on when the specific user started tweeting or when they joined Twitter..
for i,tweet in enumerate(sntwitter.TwitterSearchScraper('from:AdelAljubeir since:2015-01-01 until:2021-03-14').get_items()):
    tweets_list1.append([tweet.date, tweet.id, tweet.content, tweet.user.username, tweet.lang, tweet.replyCount, tweet.retweetCount, tweet.likeCount, tweet.source, tweet.url])

# Creating a dataframe from the tweets list above
tweets_df1 = pd.DataFrame(tweets_list1, columns=['Datetime', 'Tweet Id', 'Text', 'Username', 'Language', 'Replies', 'Retweets','Likes', 'Device','Link'])


print(tweets_df1)
#Converting the data frame into an Excel sheet
tweets_df1.to_csv('C:/Users/ausit/twitterData/AdelAljubeir.csv', encoding='utf-8-sig', index = True)
```

Code 3 - Adel Al Jubeir

King Salman (@kingsalman)

```
import snscrape.modules.twitter as sntwitter    #snscrape is a Python library that bypasses Twitter's API to get as many or all tweets from a user, It is essentially a webscraper
import pandas as pd                              #pandas is a Python library used for data analysis and manipulation

# Environment--------
#must have Python 3.8 on your laptop
#pip install pandas tweepy
#snscrape from github link.. as in, pip install git+https://snscrape.git
#replace the 'from:' field with wanted users and dates next to it
#for more information on what kind of data to get using snscrape, search "snscrape modules"

# Creating list to append tweet data to
tweets_list1 = []

# Using TwitterSearchScraper to scrape data and append tweets to list
# Here we loop thorugh the searchScraper module to get the retrieved tweets and append them to a list
#We try to get as much information as possible, including the tweet's date, language, replies, likes, retweets, device source, and the tweet ID
#We have the since: and until: options to specify the dates we want, which is dependent on when the specific user started tweeting or when they joined Twitter..
for i,tweet in enumerate(sntwitter.TwitterSearchScraper('from:Kingsalman since:2015-01-01 until:2021-03-14').get_items()):
    tweets_list1.append([tweet.date, tweet.id, tweet.content, tweet.user.username, tweet.lang, tweet.replyCount, tweet.retweetCount, tweet.likeCount, tweet.source, tweet.url])

# Creating a dataframe from the tweets list above
tweets_df1 = pd.DataFrame(tweets_list1, columns=['Datetime', 'Tweet Id', 'Text', 'Username', 'Language', 'Replies', 'Retweets','Likes', 'Device','Link'])

print(tweets_df1)
#Converting the data frame into an Excel sheet
tweets_df1.to_csv('C:/Users/ausit/twitterData/Kingsalman.csv', encoding='utf-8-sig', index = True)
```

Code 4 - King Salman

Abdallah Bin Zayed (@ABZayed)

```
import snscrape.modules.twitter as sntwitter    #snscrape is a Python library that bypasses Twitter's API to get as many or all tweets from a user. It is essentially a webscraper
import pandas as pd                              #pandas is a Python library used for data analysis and manipulation

# Environment--------
#must have Python 3.8 on your laptop
#pip install pandas tweepy
#snscrape from github link.. as in, pip install git+https://snscrape.git
#replace the 'from:' field with wanted users and dates next to it
#for more information on what kind of data to get using snscrape, search "snscrape modules"

# Creating list to append tweet data to
tweets_list1 = []

# Using TwitterSearchScraper to scrape data and append tweets to list
# Here we loop thorugh the searchScraper module to get the retrieved tweets and append them to a list
#We try to get as much information as possible, including the tweet's date, language, replies, likes, retweets, device source, and the tweet ID
#We have the since: and until: options to specify the dates we want, which is dependent on when the specific user started tweeting or when they joined Twitter..
for i,tweet in enumerate(sntwitter.TwitterSearchScraper('from:ABZayed since:2015-01-01 until:2021-03-14').get_items()):
    tweets_list1.append([tweet.date, tweet.id, tweet.content, tweet.user.username, tweet.lang, tweet.replyCount, tweet.retweetCount, tweet.likeCount, tweet.source, tweet.url])

# Creating a dataframe from the tweets list above
tweets_df1 = pd.DataFrame(tweets_list1, columns=['Datetime', 'Tweet Id', 'Text', 'Username', 'Language', 'Replies', 'Retweets','Likes', 'Device','Link'])

print(tweets_df1)
#Converting the data frame into an Excel sheet
tweets_df1.to_csv('C:/Users/ausit/twitterData/ABZayed.csv', encoding='utf-8-sig', index = True)
```

Code 5 - Abdallah Bin Zayed

All tweets from 01-01-2015 to 13-04-2021 were extracted to separate .cvs files. The reasons for capturing the tweets for such a long timeline are two-folds: (1) to make sure all the samples are obtained within the same, identified timespan, (2) to offset the discrepancy in the frequency of tweeting; for instance, the (n=18) isn't necessarily obtainable for a narrow timespan since the actors chosen have significantly different tweeting frequencies and may not all have tweeted 18 times within the chosen timespan. Expanding the timeline allows access to a large data set, guaranteeing the comfortable and selective access to (n=18) for each of the accounts. The Tweets were not translated within this study because the data set contains a link to the original Tweet, where the Tweet is automatically translated and avoids the author's bias. However, I must warn that the google translations for most of the Tweets were alarmingly inadequate and failed to capture the essence and message of Tweet consistently.

The Tweet sample of (n=18) were chosen according to the researcher's judgment of the most noteworthy tweets. These samples were chosen after the researcher's familiarization with a very large sample of the Twitter handles and an even larger sample of Tweets from the Arab Twittersphere. This followed an initial analysis of the data that guided the judgment of the researcher to select the specific (n=18) for each Twitter handle that will be a part of this study. After the (n=18) Tweets were selected for each Twitter handle, they were merged together in one file (which will be made available for review as well). For these (n=18), content analysis was performed. Content analysis is a research method often employed in the humanities and social sciences. It is a method which allows for systematically reviewing texts, media works, pictures, books or any other form of information that is not direct human interaction. To perform content analysis, the information within the text is coded or broken down to meaningful elements. This is to maintain the validity and replicability of the research. According to Berelson, content analysis is used to identify the emotional state of the writer, identify the intention of the message, identify the focus and patterns in communication and reveals propaganda (55). Even though codes or parameters have been developed to analyze the sample, the researcher does not claim that this study follows the framework method because the Framework method is more associated with deductive reasoning, while this study falls more closely towards inductive reasoning, where the proposed classification framework itself was developed after following Twitter diplomats and making observations.

The advantage of using content analysis is: (1) it can produce both quantitative and qualitative data, (2) it highlights cultural and linguistic meaningful patterns that is difficult to capture otherwise, (3) can be used to develop categories which can form the basis of machine learning software to produce automated categorizations, (4) is an obstructive means of obtaining data, and (5) provides an opportunity to decode important insights that can only be highlighted by observation.

Developing the Parameters

The Parameters that been developed to guide through the reflexive thematic content analysis are as follows:

Parameter	Name	Description
1	Direct Mention	Direct mention of recognizable names of actors or group of actors
2	Implied Mention	Implied reference to an actor or group of actors through reasonable implication, commonly accepted alternative names and adjectives, or as the committer of a specific act.

3	Language	Language. The choice of language of tweets naturally provides an automatic identification of who the target audience is to a certain extent
4	References	Use of group-specific references such as religious references, cultural references, language-specific references, folklore or any other reference that loses its coherence in translation
5	Location	Use of a location tag or explicit mention of a location or a location-specific entity or phenomena

Table 2 - Parameters

Parameter 1 – Direct Mention is the explicit mention of a recognizable name of actor or a group of actors. The mention can be in the form of a 'mention' which is a function that Twitter makes available for users, or in the form of a hashtag or plain texts.

Parameter 2 – Implied Mention is the implicit mention of an actor or a group of actors within the Tweet. Implied mentions are dependent on the reader's ability to make the necessary connections within the Tweet that hint to the implied actors. Parameter 2 captures the complexity of Tweets which mirrors the complexity of human-to-human communication, which is a main reason that disallows reducing messages in a Tweet to codes that can be used to automatically interpret the text. For instance, the Tweet could contain not only implicit reference to the actor but can refer to the actor through even more cloaked and difficult to decode alternative names or adjectives such as 'the killers,' 'the strong man,' 'the Saffah,' 'the fire worshippers,' 'the Bedouins,' and so on.

Parameter 3 – Language is a straightforward indication of who the twitter diplomat is trying to communicate with the most. Yet, emphasis should be placed on the *most*. It's not so obvious that a Tweet in Hebrew for a Twitter Diplomat who's aware that a majority of his/her followers are Arabs is necessarily a Tweet that is speaking predominantly to a Jewish audience. Here, the complexity of Twitter communication is once again apparent.

Parameter 4 – References are the mentions within a tweet that have relevance to a group of people and could be cultural, religious, linguistic or historical. These group-specific references often lose their coherence and potency upon translation. They provide a clear indication on who the twitter diplomat is trying to appeal to, because chances are no one outside of this group will be able to identify the references. Parameter 4 allows for targeted communication and does allow for the undetected communication of certain messages as well.

Parameter 5 – Location is reference to a specific location. This reference can be done by using the location tag or by including the name of the location in the text or a location-specific phenomena.

Consider the following examples:

عبدالله بن زايد
@ABZayed
الإمارات العربية المتحدة حساب حكومي رسمي

رافق أستاذنا زكي نسيبة الشيخ زايد و كان مترجمه الخاص و صديقه
وهبه الله عقلا راجحا وقلبا كبيرا.. أديب الدبلوماسية و رائد من رواد الثقافة و التنوير في الإمارات..
شكرا لعطائك و محبتك و تعليمك
@Zakinus

Translate Tweet

10:26 PM · Feb 11, 2021 · Twitter for iPhone

316 Retweets 9 Quote Tweets 994 Likes

Tweet 13 - Example on Parameter applications

This Tweet n contains parameter 1 – direct mention of Zaki Nuseibah twice, once in text and once in a mention. It also contains parameter 4 – reference to a historically and culturally relevant group-specific figure, Sheikh Zayed and parameter 5 – location with reference to the UAE.

عبدالله بن زايد
@ABZayed
الإمارات العربية المتحدة حساب حكومي رسمي

نجوى كرم - زايد مجدها via youtu.be/9ev1Y9AeL1I @YouTube

Translate Tweet

Najwa Karam - Zayed Majedha [Official Video] (2021) / زايد - ...
Najwa Karam - Zayed Majedha [Official Video] (2021) / نجوى كرم - زايد مجدهاLyrics By: Roger FeghaliComposed By: Antoin...
youtube.com

12:00 PM · Jan 11, 2021 · Twitter for iPhone

654 Retweets 45 Quote Tweets 2,205 Likes

Tweet 14 - Example on Parameter applications

This Tweet contains parameter 4 – reference to a group-specific folklore by sharing a video link to a famous Lebanese singer which contains the title of the founder of the UAE Sheikh Zayed. Both of these references would be difficult to identify or relate to for non-Arabic speaking audiences.

The parameters have been developed to guide the categorization of the Tweets along with the proposed categorization framework. Furthermore, it provides a future basis for the development of codes that can help identify the category of each tweet, by training software to map out correlations between the Tweet parameter and Tweet category. It is expected for them to provide an error-ridden guidance system towards further improvements and eventually the development of automatic categorization. In their current format, the developed parameters do not provide a conclusive indication of which category each tweet should be categorized at. The categorization – at this stage – requires the researcher's judgment and justification for placing each tweet in a specific category while making use of the parameters to assist in the categorization, by providing a breakdown of the noteworthy components within a Tweet.

Conclusion

This chapter attempted to provide sufficient details on the steps that guided the process, without alienating the interdisciplinary or general reader. It started with a clear and concise research question that had been earlier mentioned in passing in a preceding section. It then proceeded to guide the reader on some of the main steps undertaken for manipulating the secondary data published by

Twiplomacy that allowed further familiarization with the Arab Twittersphere. Some of the trends found served as guidance for the choice of the 4 case studies selected. After the selection of the 4 case studies, the codes written and executed to extract the relevant Tweets are included. Then, the chapter outlines the parameters developed to guide the categorization. The chapter closes with presenting two examples on how the parameters can be allotted to each Tweet. In the next Chapter, the results and main findings will be outlined.

Chapter 6:
Findings

Introduction

This chapter produces a display of the findings of the question asked in Chapter 5, in what is a hopefully meaningful way to the reader. Chapter 5 raised the question of 'who are Arab state-actors tweeting for?' and in the pursuit of answering that question, the researcher had to ask if there were any main trends within the Arab Twittersphere worth noting from available secondary data. The first part of the Findings presents the trends that have been identified within the Arab Twittersphere. The second part of the Findings section proceeds to present the results for the Research Question that was originally raised by this research after selecting 4

Chapter objectives:

6.1 Trends within the Arab Twittersphere:

- Most followed Arab state-actors
- Most amplified Arab state-actors
- Most conversed to Arab state-actors
- Most addressed Arab state-actors

6.2 Who are Arab state-actors tweeting for?

- Abdallah Bin Zayed
- Adel Al Jubeir
- King Salman
- Mohamed Bin Rashid

specific Arab state-actors, extracting archived Tweets for a unified timeline, singling out a sample of (n=18) for each Twitter Diplomat, identifying the parameters present within each Tweet and finally categorizing it.

Trends within the Arab Twittersphere

As expected, trends do exist within the Arab Twittersphere. The most compelling of which are almost all unexpected. Below are snapshots of some of these trends presented in the form of '10-most' lists that attempt to highlight to the reader a few of the trends within the Arab Twittersphere.

Most followed State-actors in the Arab Twittersphere

This list shows the most followed state-actors within the Arab Twittersphere. It includes a count of the Twitter diplomats' followers, to justify the ranking. Queen Rania Al Abdullah of Jordan (@QueenRania) tops the list with 10,435,132 followers. Queen Rania has consistently been ranked as the most followed state-actor in the Arab Twittersphere, for as long as she has been present on the Twittersphere. This is quite telling. To have the most followed state-actor in the Arab Twittersphere be not a celebratory, cosmetic state-actor that isn't a state-actor at all in a final analysis is a little unusual. Are Arab publics looking for the social side of the political? Indeed, Queen Rania's bio introduces her as "a mum and a wife with a really cool day job." This along with her self-expressive Tweets in the past highlights the personal side of being a state-actor or a state-sanctioned actor. Which is apparently consistently well received. The second most followed state-actor on the Arab Twittersphere is Sheikh Mohammed Bin Rashid of Dubai (@HHShkMohd) coming in as a very close-second with 10,201,675 followers. Sheikh Mohamed, or more commonly known as MBR, is the Vice President of the UAE and the ruler of Dubai. MBR is all kinds of unique. For instance, MBR is considered as the architect of the 'city of hope' to disenfranchised Arab publics. Dubai – the most iconic city of the UAE – has time and again has served as the city of example to most states of the Arab world. It's a city that was built in less than 50 years and has had tremendous successes in a wide range of categories. The UAE has consistently been voted as the country most Arab youth would like to immigrate to. This places MBR in a unique position of soft-power that is based on progression and innovation in the Arab world. Third on the list is King Salman Bin Abdel Aziz, king of Saudi Arabia with 8,221,159 followers. King Salman is also in a unique place in Arabian geopolitics. Yet a very different type of unique that MBR. As the custodian of the two holy mosques King Salman automatically claims an almost naturally transnational audience, receptive of messages about the pilgrims, the two holy mosques or general religion-specific messages. King Salman was also ranked by Twiplomacy as the most effective world leader on Twitter in 2018 (56). Effectiveness is a measure of the number of retweets per tweet. In 2020, however the most effective world leader on Twitter was Donald Trump who had an average of

24,000 retweets/tweet, leaving (@KingSalman) at a very close second who had an average of 23,537 retweets/tweet. Yet, with the recent de-platforming of Donald Trump, King Salman automatically claims back the title of 'most effective world leader on Twitter.' This basically means that Tweets from King Salman really matter. Both King Salman and Mohammed Bin Rashid made the 'true reach' list of leaders on Twitter and were the only Arab state-actors to have made the list. The True reach list is the percentage of followers that Tweets actually reach. King Salman had a true reach of 65% of his followers, while Mohamed Bin Rashid had a true reach of 45% of his followers. The Fourth most followed Arab state-actor is Abdallah Bin Zayed (@ABZayed), the foreign minister of the UAE with 4,636,513. To have a foreign minister outrank multiple state-leaders that are often national icons is very curious. It means someone is listening to ABZ. Is it international audiences that he is leading public diplomacy efforts with, is it national audiences that somehow decided that his tweets are more important to see than MBZ's (the crown prince of UAE and de-facto leader), or is it a transnational pan-Arab audience? All questions worth investigating. Yet for now, there certainly is the sense that ABZ leaves quite an impression on the Arab Twittersphere. Furthermore, Abdallah Bin Zayed has consistently been ranked as the most followed foreign minister in the world by Twiplomacy (54). This further reinforces that ABZ seems to be well-regarded in multiple networks on the Twittersphere. Egypt's Abdel Fattah El Sisi ranks as the 5th most followed state-actor, a rank well-worth investigating. The reason for that is the clear trend of the absence of El Sisi on any other popularity or soft-power indicators. Why is ElSisi so well-followed, then becomes a very natural question. The UAE's Mohamed Bin Zayed rank at number 6 on the most followed state-actors in the Arab Twittersphere. The ranking of MBZ as the lagging behind El Sisi sheds further doubt on the appropriateness of El Sisi as the 6th most followed state-actor on the Arab Twittersphere. This is because the influence and popularity of MBZ far exceeds El Sisi, in the offline world. Yet, what MBZ's ranking does reveal is the lack of investment in a strategic Twitter Diplomacy communication plan, and is not an indication of his geopolitical influence. 7th on the list is surprisingly the Turkish president Recep Erdogan with a personal Twitter handle dedicated to the Arabic language (@rterdogan_ar) with 2,940,985 followers. The presence of a non-Arab state-actor and his ranking as one of the most followed state-actor accounts is very telling. It tells of a detailed and targeted public diplomacy campaign aimed at Arab youth. The 8th most followed state-actor on the Arab Twittersphere is the Saudi MOFA's account. It's not clear what the presence of the Saudi MOFA on the top-10 list indicates because it requires a detailed qualitative analysis of its Tweets. The unusualness of the presence of the Saudi MOFA on the top-10 list is the well-recorded ineffectiveness of most MOFAs to successfully utilize Twitter Diplomacy. It could be an indicator of an extensive public diplomacy campaign, a vast awareness campaign aimed at citizens to gain their support, network with diplomats or communicate with citizens abroad. The 9th on the list is Jordan's King Abdullah, who is preceded by his wife by a factor of 9. The difference between the ranking of Queen Rania and that of King Abdullah is peculiar because supposedly they are playing for the same team. Furthermore, to be outranked by a foreign state-actor tweeting in a foreign language, a MOFA that broke a global tradition of inefficacy of MFAs, a state-leader that came to power through a military coup that ousted Egypt's first democratically elected leader is indicative of a serious soft-power deficit or a serious lack of investment in a deliberate Twitter Diplomacy communication plan. And finally, tenth on the list is the American MOFA, with an Arabic dedicated Twitter handle (@USAbilAraby). Once again, this captures the presence of one more non-Arab state-actor in the top-10 list.

What is missing from the Twitter Diplomacy data set is Adel Al Jubeir (@AdelAljubeir) – Foreign Minister of Saudi Arabia who has 3.1M followers. Had Adel Al Jubeir been a part of the Twitter Diplomacy data, he would have ranked as the 7th most followed state-actor in the Arab Twittersphere, and the second most followed foreign minister globally.

An important consideration for the top-10 most followed list is that it could be thought of as an equivalent to "whose story is most likely to win." This is because Twitter Diplomats with more followers are in a unique position to shape the agenda in their networks and frame them successfully with their version of the story. And hence to have the most likely story to win and shape the narrative on the Arab Twittersphere be a cosmetic state-actor's is telling of the lack of compelling stories.

Twitter Handle	Verified Names	Followers
QueenRania	Rania Al Abdullah	10435132
HHShkMohd	HH Sheikh Mohammed	10201675
KingSalman	سلمان بن عبدالعزيز	8221159
ABZayed	عبدالله بن زايد	4636513
AlsisiOfficial	Abdelfattah Elsisi	3742418
MohamedBinZayed	محمد بن زايد	3503296
rterdogan_ar	رجب طيب أردوغان	2940985
KSAMOFA	وزارة الخارجية	2629918
KingAbdullahII	عبدالله بن الحسين	1759272
USAbilAraby	الخارجية الأمريكية	1172041

Table 3 - Most followed state-actors in the Arab Twittersphere

Most amplified state-actors in the Arab Twittersphere

The most amplified state-actors in the Arab Twittersphere are an indication of who is most visible within the political narrative of the Arab Twittersphere. It is an indication of 'whose story is everywhere' or a story you are most likely to run into. It shows whose tweets are retweeted the most. It is not a measure of the average number of retweets each tweet receives, and hence not a measure of the effectiveness of the Twitter Diplomat. It can also be thought of whose influence is most obvious in trying to shape the political narrative on the Arab Twittersphere. Accordingly, the biggest influence is Iraq's former Foreign Minister Mohammed Ali Al Hakim. This is a personal influence, as he explicitly reminds his readers on his Twitter bio. The second and third biggest influence is the Emirati and the Jordanian foreign ministries,' respectively. Fourth is the influence of Abdallah Bin Zayed. A usual presence at this point in most lists. Fifth is surprisingly the Russian Government's Arabic Twitter handle. A shocking presence worth investigating. Sixth is the sitting President of Iraq, Barham Salih. Seventh is the Saudi influence, where the rest are all Jordanian influences.

Twitter Handle	Verified Names	Retweets
Maalhakim	محمد علي الحكيم	2743
MoFAICUAE	وزارة الخارجية و التعاوت الدولي	2299
ForeignMinistry	وزارة الخارجية الأردنية	2240
ABZayed	عبدالله بن زايد	2193
Russia_AR	روسيا بالعربية	1747
BarhamSalih	Barham Salih	1133
FaisalbinFarhan	فيصل بن فرحان	1084
PrimeMinistry	Prime Ministry JO	1039
OmarRazzaz	Omar Razzaz	1025
AymanHsafadi	Ayman Safadi	916

Table 4 - Most amplified state-actors in the Arab Twittersphere

Most conversed to state-actors in the Arab Twittersphere

Account	Verified Names	Replies
Presidency_Sy	Syrian Presidency	1210
IraqiGovt	Government of Iraq -الحكومة العراقية	1174
Iraqimofa	وزارة الخارجية العراقية	1006
Israelipm_ar	بينيامين نتنياهو	720
ar_khamenei	الامام الخامنئي	673
khalidalkhalifa	خالد بن أحمد	642
MohamedBinZayed	محمد بن زايد	613
USAbilAraby	الخارجية الأمريكية	604
IraqiPMO	المكتب الاعلامي لرئيس الوزراء	560
IraqiPresidency	رئاسة جمهورية العراق	461

Table 5 - Most conversed to state-actors in the Arab Twittersphere

The most conversed to state-actors in the Arab Twittersphere indicate with which state-actors are most of the conversations happening. It also shows who does the public have something to say to. Accordingly, the first state-actor that the Arab Twitter users are trying to make their comments heard to is the Syrian Presidency, commonly understood as Syria's Bashar Al Assad (@Presidency_Sy). The next most conversed with state-actor is the Government of Iraq (@IraqiGovt) and the Iraqi MOFA (@Iraqimofa). The fourth most conversed with state-actor in the Arab Twittersphere is Israel's Benjamin Netanyahu, who has dedicated an Arabic Twitter handle to reach out to Arabic speaking publics (@Israelipm_ar). The fifth most conversed to state-actor in the Arab Twittersphere is Imam Khamenei of Iran (@ar_khamenei), who also dedicated a Twitter handle that speaks exclusively Arabic. The sixth state-actor that Arabic Twitter users are trying to make their voices heard to is Bahrain's former foreign minister Khalid Khalifa (@khalidkhalifa). The seventh actor is UAE's crown prince Mohamed Bin Zayed (@MohamedBinZayed). The eighth state-actor that Arabic Twitter users are trying to converse with is the American MOFA, on its Arabic Twitter handle (@USAbilAraby). The ninth and tenth actors are Iraq's PM media office and the Iraqi Presidency.

Most addressed state-actors in the Arab Twittersphere

Account	Verified Names	Mentions
UAEmGov	حكومة الامارات الذكية	3674
USAbilAraby	الخارجية الأمريكية	3230
IraqiGovt	Government of Iraq -الحكومة العراقية	3103
maduro_ar	Nicolás Maduro	2561
grandserail	رئاسة مجلس الوزراء	1946
KSAmofaEN	Foreign Ministry	1919
HukoomiQatar	حكومي – قطر	1498
MfaEgypt	Egypt MFA Spokesperson	1485
IraqiPresidency	رئاسة جمهورية العراق	1463
ForeignMinistry	وزارة الخارجية الأردنية	1462
Iraqimofa	وزارة الخارجية العراقية	1304
AymanHsafadi	Ayman Safadi	1264

Table 6 - Most addressed state-actors in the Arab Twittersphere

The most addressed state-actors are a category synonymous to 'who makes the headlines the most' in the pre-Twitter era. It is an analysis of which state-actors on the Arab Twittersphere gets the most mentions. It does not indicate, however who the mentions are originating from. They could be originating from the Arabic Twitter users (the public) or other Twitter Diplomats. Most addressed is not the same as most conversed with; since most conversed with is a category that identifies who the Arabic Twitters users are trying to 'tell' something to. On the other hand, most addressed is similar to 'commenting' on something, without directing the speech to that actor. What I want to highlight for the purposes of this study is that the second most addressed state-actor is the American MOFA, the fourth is Brazil's Nicolas Maduro (@maduro_ar) and the sixth is the English Twitter handle of the Saudi MOFA (@KSAmofaEN).

Who is Arab state-actors Tweeting for?

Abdallah Bin Zayed

Below is the classification of ABZ's Tweets using the categorization framework developed in this thesis for n=18.Below is a quantitative analysis of the percentage of the different categories the n=18.

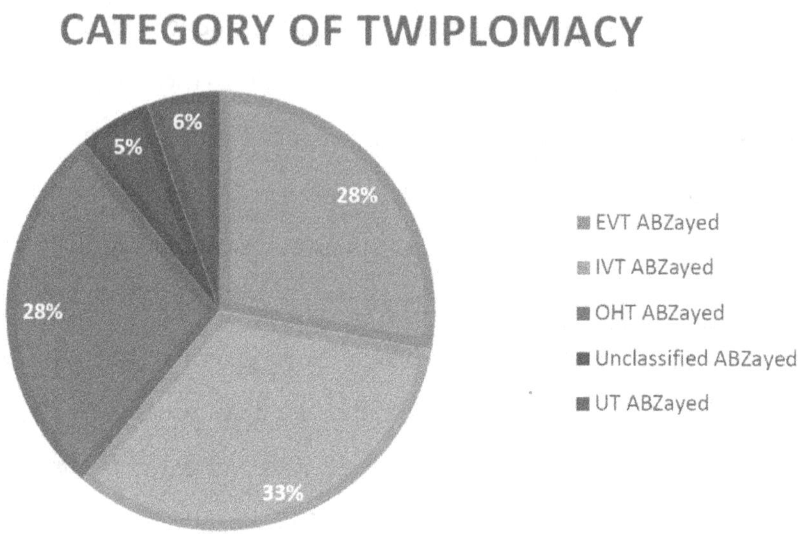

Figure 6 - ABZ

ABZ's most common Twiplomacy audience at 33% were Internal Vertical; meaning domestic audience. He practiced equal ratios of Overt Horizontal Twiplomacy with counterparts and External Vertical Twiplomacy, sitting at 28%. A new category of Twiplomacy was identified with ABZ's n17, which was addressed to the crown prince of the UAE, MBZ. This category of Twiplomacy was called 'Upper Twiplomacy.' Categorizing ABZ's tweets was quite challenging at times, because of the lack of clear parameters in some of his tweets. This resulted in uncategorized tweets, which are thought to be mainly self-expression (e.g.: n8). He was the most state-actor to engage in self-expressive tweets.

The discovery that ABZ engages mostly in IVT wasn't as per the expectation of his Twiplomacy strategy, because the main expectation was that a Foreign Minister would be more concerned with OHT or EVT.

Adel Al Jubeir

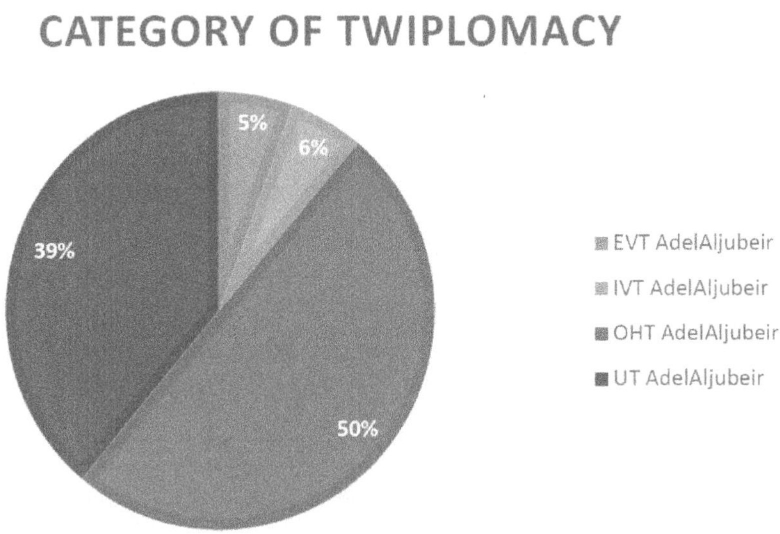

Figure 7 - Adel Al Jubeir

Adel Al Jubeir displayed a substantial amount of OHT, sitting at 50% – as per expected. Not only that, he engages mostly with diplomatic actors within his same government. One of the most interesting findings within Adel Al Jubeir's Twiplomacy patterns is the identification of a new type of twiplomacy: Upper Twiplomacy. He displayed the highest levels of UT in the samples, sitting at a whopping 39%. Direct speech to public was the least used Twiplomacy pattern that he displayed, for both internal publics and external, sitting at 6% and 5%, respectively.

It was expected that Adel Al Jubeir will display a very high level of OHT – as he is a central node to the twiplomatic network, but the unexpected finding was the emergence of a new type of Twiplomacy category which had to be developed because of the reoccurrence of the UT twiplomatic tweets.

King Salman

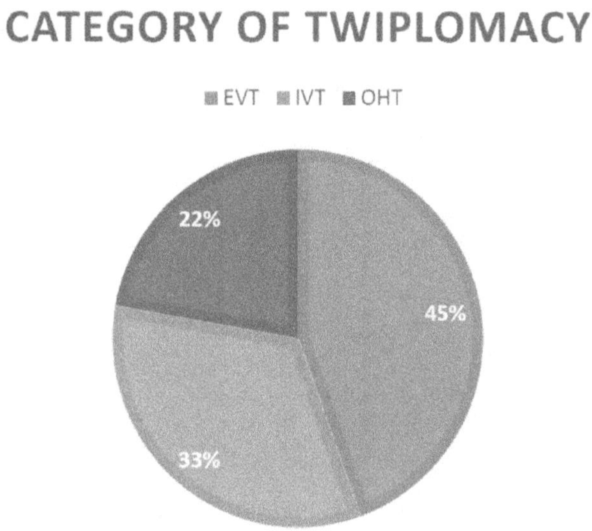

Figure 8 - King Salman

King Salman represents one of the most peculiar and interesting case studies in Twiplomacy. He is in a very unique position within the Arab and Islamic worlds, where he often speaks directly to both these publics or about them. This makes his categorization Internal if the reference point was the Islamic identity or the Arab one. Yet, because this thesis has operationalized the state as the fixed reference point for all the case studies, it made Arabic and Islamic publics external. Hence, King Salman's most common twiplomatic efforts were EVT, sitting at a whopping 45%. Which proves that he is indeed in a very unique position to directly engage almost naturally with the Arabic and Islamic publics. He also displayed direct speech to his own citizens at a ratio of 33%. Finally, he displayed OHT at a ratio of 22%.

Mohamed Bin Rashid

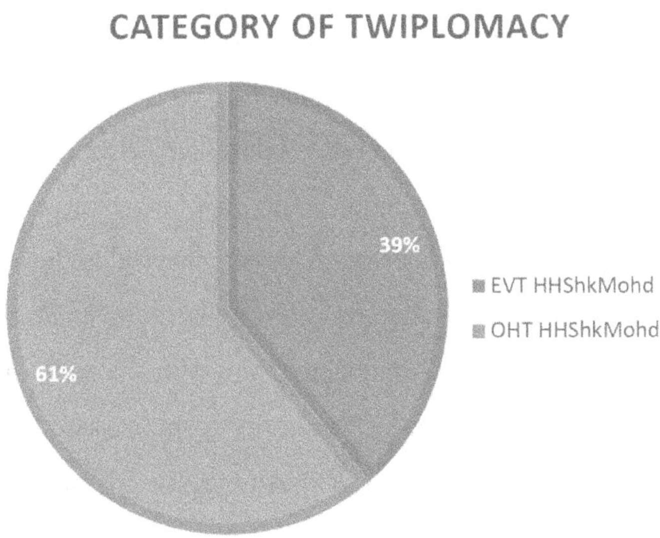

Figure 9 - MBR

MBR to the Arabic Twittersphere is what Obama is to the American one; he's the best. MBR showed two main types of Twiplomacy categories; OHT at 61% and EVT at 39%. What is interesting is that he did not engage in any form of UT to the state-head of the UAE. In fact, his tweets that included the mention of MBZ were brotherly and friendly, without reference to him as a superior or trying to prove loyalty. What is also noteworthy is the lack of IVT within his tweets. It seems that they have been replaced for either EVT to the entire Arab or Islamic nations or EVT to foreign publics.

The general result is that 3 of the 4 Arab state-actors studied used Twiplomacy mostly to connect with diplomatic counter-parts (OHT), except peculiarly the most followed foreign minister in the world; ABZ, who displayed a higher level of IVT than OHT.

Discussion

An important finding within this study is the hesitation detected by Arab state-actors when addressing citizens of another nation. It was very uncommon for an Arab state-actor to openly address the people of another state. Tweets that did address citizens of another nation usually were carefully accompanied by direct speeches to the respective state-actors and were carefully delivered as a social nicety. Yet, all state-actors demonstrated a level of comfort in addressing Islamic and Arabic publics or *the Umma.* King Salman was, by far, the most optimally positioned to naturally speak to Arabic and Islamic publics as a routine part of most of his tweets. This can be clearly thought of as a completely effortless public diplomacy effort, securing the prestige of the Saudi nation within the Arabic and Islamic nations. This was further reinforced by recurring direct speeches to ‘the pilgrims’ and direct speeches on religious days. MBR, on the other hand, also demonstrated a very high level of comfort in addressing Arabic and Islamic people, yet it was more deliberate and well-orchestrated, with clear takeaways. The level of public diplomacy demonstrated by MBR was the most sophisticated, clearly indicating a higher level of soft-power and strategic Twiplomacy efforts. Another interesting finding within this research was the practice and concept of Upper Twiplomacy – which was identified as a Twiplomacy effort toward a superior. UT was very prevalent mostly with Adel Al Jubeir. Adel Al Jubeir almost never spoke directly to any public, even his own. While ABZ did.

In general, all 4 state-actors were more concerned with diplomatic communication with counter-parts than with engaging with vertical Twiplomacy. This is reinforced by their absence from the 10 most-addressed Arab state actors and the most conversed with, as well, indicating that Arab Twitter users are not trying to deliver their messages to them and are not 'commenting' on their actions. Even though it is accepted that most conversed with or most addressed isn't automatically indication of the favorability of an actor to Twitter users, but it is an indication of the level of engagement and interaction with the actor. Which is one of the main goals of delivering messages from a two-way platform. Similarly, only ABZ made it to the most amplified list, indicating that his influence on trying to shape the political narrative by guaranteeing higher visibility is higher than the other 3 state-actors studied.

A very interesting finding within this study is the hard to ignore visibility of non-Arab state-actors. Automatically, all non-Arab state actors are engaging in EVT when dedicating a channel specifically for Arab audiences. This means non-Arab state actors are engaging in highly intentional, rigorous public diplomacy programs competing for the attention of Arab Twitter users, while the Arab publics are not being targeted by either their own states or a fellow Arab-state. This is a huge lost opportunity for Arab-state actors to engage their own publics, without realizing the tough competition already ahead of them in engaging their own publics.

Recommended Research

The natural next step for this study is to be able to automate the categorization of each Tweet using software. This was the main reason for developing the 5 parameters. The 5 parameters were developed to serve as the ground work for attempting to train software to automatically categorize Tweets. Machine learning can be applied to any developed set of codes with clear parameters and an already categorized sample. The challenge for now is mapping patterns of how the parameters and the final category of the Tweet relate to each other. With mathematical precision, that is. The mapping and extraction of any patterns can itself only be done through software. After the extraction of patterns of relations between the parameters and the Tweets, machine learning can be applied to train software to automatically categorize any Tweet. There are no challenges in writing such a code for English language Tweets (even though it has not been done yet). Yet, the Arabic language contains far more complications in writing a code that can take into account the complexities of the language. Hence, such a project will be completely novel for both fields (even in English). Such a software could be highly useful in automatically identifying social media political weapons, i.e.: twitter handles with an above average ratio of EVT – which will signify interference in a sovereign state, highly vigorous public diplomacy campaigns by foreign states or terrorist organization recruitment campaigns. Furthermore, another area of research that should be investigated is the non-Arab state-actors within the Arab Twittersphere, as the study consistently reveals. It was observed that multiple non-Arab state actors do exist within the Arabic Twittersphere. A qualitative analysis of their tweets is overdue. Similarly, a mapping of the Arab Twittersphere is also overdue, which would include the first adopters of Twiplomacy, the most followed, the most informational, with more in-depth analysis that this study has been able to provide and including the full (n=125) sample. A further area of research that can be investigated is what kind of Twiplomacy category do unstable states mostly utilize?

Conclusion

What we don't know about Twiplomacy can fill a lot of books. Within the scope of the time allocated for this research – the main conclusion has been that the Arab Twittersphere contains a million uninvestigated phenomena simmering and bubbling underneath the surface. One of them was understanding who Arab-state actors are talking to in their tweets. The main findings of this study were that the categorization framework was indeed useful in providing guidance on who is the audience of the Twiplomat and can be applied to other Twiplomats more broadly. It also outlined that 3 out of the 4 studied Twiplomats used Twiplomacy to connect with diplomatic counter-parts, where only one displayed a higher level of attempt to engage with publics. It also outlined the hesitation of the studied accounts to engage in public diplomacy efforts or any form of engagement to Arab publics of a different state. Most engagement with foreign publics of a neighboring Arab states were accompanied by explicit mention of that Arab states' actors or directing speech to 'Arabic and Islamic Umma.' Furthermore, it is evident that there is fierce competition on the attention of Arab public on the Twittersphere by non-Arab state actors. While the same is being missed by state-actors. Another finding within this study is the formation of a new category 'Upper Twiplomacy' which is using Twiplomacy reaffirm loyalty to the state, which was significantly prevalent.

Bibliography

1. **The washington post.** *Jordan announces gag order on Prince Hamzah investigation after new recording is leaked.* 2021.

2. **Smith, Janet.** *Dust or Dew: Immortality in the Ancient Near East and in Psalm 49.* 2010.

3. *Twiplomacy in the age of Donald Trump: Is the diplomatic code changing?* **Simunjak, Maja and Caliandro, Alessandro.** 2019, The information society .

4. **Marks, Sally and Freeman, Chas. W.** *Diplomacy.* s.l. : Encyclopædia Britannica, 2020.

5. **Cull, Nicholas.** *Public Diplomacy and Soft Power: Government, People and Foreign Policy.* 23 June 2015.

6. *Public diplomacy networks: China's public diplomacy communication practices in twitter during Two Sessions.* **Jia, Ruixue and Li, Weidong.** 1, 2020, Public Relations Review, Vol. 46.

7. *The Development of Pan-Arab Broadcasting Under Authoritarian Regimes — A Comparison of Sawt al-Arab ("Voice of the Arabs") and Al Jazeera News Channel.* **Musleh-Motut, Nawal.** s.l. : ProQuest Dissertations Publishing, 2006.

8. **Wikipedia.** Voice of the Arabs. [Online] https://en.wikipedia.org/wiki/Voice_of_the_Arabs.

9. *Refugee Status in the Arab and Islamic Tradition: A Comparative Study of Jiwar, Aman and the 1951 Geneva Convention Relating to the*

Status of Refugees. **Shoukri, Arafat Madi.** s.l. : ProQuest dissertations publishings, 2008.

10. *Understanding Pashtunwali and the Manifestation of Pashtun Nationalism in Pakistan: A Conceptual Analysis.* **Khan, Surat, Faheem, Muhammad and Gul, Saima.** 1, s.l. : Global Social Sciences Review (GSSR), 2019, Vol. 4.

11. **Berridge, G.R.** *Diplomacy - Theory and Practice.* 2nd. 2002.

12. **Buzan, Barry, Wæver, Ole and Wilde, Jaap de.** *Security: A New Framework for Analysis.* 1998.

13. **WHO.** *Timeline: WHO's COVID-19 response.* 2020.

14. *Turkey's Twitter public diplomacy: Towards a "new" cult of personality.* **Uysal, Nur and Schroeder, Jared.** 5, 2019, Public Relations Review, Vol. 45.

15. *Public relations message strategies and public diplomacy 2.0: An empirical analysis using Central-Eastern European and Western Embassy Twitter accounts.* **D.Dodd, Melissa and J.Collins, Steve.** 2, 2017, Public Relations Review, Vol. 43.

16. *Friend, Ally, or Rival? Twitter Diplomacy as Technosocial Performance of National Identity.* **Shahin, Saif and Huang, Q. Elyse.** 2019, International Journal of Communication, Vol. 13.

17. *Twitter and the Challenges of Digital.* **Duncombe, Constance.** 2018, SAIS Review of International Affairs.

18. *International Organisations on Social Media 2017.* **Twiplomacy.** 2017.

19. *Twitter and the Challenges of Digital Diplomacy.* **Duncombe, Constance.** 2, 2018, The SAIS Review of International Affairs, Vol. 38.

20. *Towards prestige mobility? Diplomatic prestige and digital diplomacy.* **Manor, Ilan and Pamment, James.** 2, 2019, Cambridge review of International Affairs, Vol. 32.

21. **Takhteyev, Yuri, Wellman, Barry and Gruzd, Anatoliy.** How Twitter Makes the Internet More Local - Social Media Isn't As Global As One Might Think. [Online] April 4 2012. https://www.foreign affairs.com / articles / 2012-04-04/how-twitter-makes-internet-more-local.

22. **Ferguson, Niall.** The False Prophecy of Hyperconnection - How to Survive the Networked Age. [Online] 2017. https://www.foreign affairs.com/articles/2017-08-15/false-prophecy-hyperconnection.

23. **Wikiepdia.** [Online] https://en.wikipedia.org/wiki/There_are_known_knowns#cite_note-defense.gov-transcript-1.

24. **Chertoff, Michael and Rasmussen, Anders Fogh.** The Unhackable Election - What It Takes to Defend Democracy. [Online] 2019. https://www.foreignaffairs.com/articles/2018-12-11/unhackable -election.

25. **Rosenberger, Jamie M. Fly and Laura.** How Silicon Valley Can Protect U.S. Democracy - A Proactive Approach to Guarding Against Russian Meddling. [Online] 22 February 2018. foreignaffairs.com/ articles / united-states/2018-02-22 / how-silicon-valley-can-protect-us-democracy.

26. **Albright, Jonathan.** Trolls on Twitter: How Mainstream and Local News Outlets Were Used to Drive a Polarized News Agenda - Fake accounts, real news? [Online] 16 February 2018. https://medium.com /berkman - klein - center / trolls-on-twitter-how-mainstream-and-local-news-outlets-were-used-to-drive-a-polarized-news-agenda-e8b514e4a 37a.

27. **Rosenberger, Laura.** China's Coronavirus Information Offensive - Beijing Is Using New Methods to Spin the Pandemic to Its

advantadge. [Online] 2020. https://www.foreignaffairs.com/articles/china/2020-04-22/chinas-coronavirus-information-offensive.

28. **Jeffrey, James.** Is Twitter Hurting Ethiopia? Rumor and Unrest in a Fragile Federation. [Online] 7 November 2016. https://www.foreignaffairs.com/articles/ethiopia/2016-11-07/twitter-hurting-ethiopia.

29. **Liao, Rebecca.** Digital Diplomacy - In China, the Tech Industry Does What Washington Can't. [Online] 2015. https://www.foreignaffairs.com/articles/china/2015-10-12/digital-diplomacy.

30. **Kamarava, Mehran.** *The modern Middle East - A Political History since the First World War.* s.l.: University of California Press, 2005.

31. **Twitter.** Permanent Suspension of @realDonaldTrump. [Online] 2021. https:// blog.twitter.com / en_us / topics / company / 2020 /suspension.html.

32. **Guardian, The.** [Online] 2021. https://www.theguardian.com/us-news/2021/jan/06/facebook-twitter-youtube-trump-video-supporters-capitol.

33. **DiResta, Renee and Stamos, Alex.** The Insurrection Hiding in Plain Sight - How Thousands of Americans Were Convinced to Storm the Capitol—and What Comes Next. [Online] 2021. https://www.foreignaffairs.com / articles / united-states / 2021-01-14 / insurrection-hiding-plain-sight.

34. **Kornbluh, Karen.** The Internet's Lost Promise - And how America can restore it. [Online] 2018. https://www.foreignaffairs.com/articles/world/2018-08-13/internets-lost-promise.

35. **Soldatov, Andrei and Borogan, Irina.** Putin Trolls Facebook - Privacy and Moscow's New Data Laws. [Online] 2015. https://www.foreignaffairs.com/articles/russian-federation/2015-11-03/putin-trolls-facebook.

36. **Slaughter, Anne-Marie.** How to Succeed in the Networked World - A Grand Strategy for the Digital Age. [Online] 2016. https://www.foreignaffairs.com/articles/world/2016-10-04/how-succeed-networked-world.

37. **Soldatov, Andrei.** Why Russia Might Shut Off the Internet - The Kremlin's Long Obsession With Central Control. [Online] 29 March 2019. https://www.foreignaffairs.com/articles/russian-federation/2019-03-29/why-russia-might-shut-internet.

38. **Tworek, Heidi.** How Germany Is Tackling Hate Speech - New Legislation Targets U.S. Social Media Companies. [Online] 2017. https://www. foreignaffairs.com / articles / germany/2017-05-16/how-germany-tackling-hate-speech.

39. *After Egypt: The Limits and Promise of Online Challenges to the Authoritarian Arab State.* **Lynch, March.** 2, 2011, Perspectives on Politics, Vol. 9.

40. **Gladwell, Malcolm.** Small Change - Why the revolution will not be tweeted. [Online] 27 September 2010. https://www.newyorker.com/magazine/2010/10/04/small-change-malcolm-gladwell.

41. **Wright, Nicholas.** How Artificial Intelligence Will Reshape the Global Order - The Coming Competition Between Digital Authoritarianism and Liberal Democracy. [Online] 2018. https://www. foreignaffairs.com/articles / world / 2018-07-10/how-artificial-intelligence-will-reshape-global-order.

42. **Pew Research Center - Journalism & Media.** The Role of Social Media in the Arab Uprisings. [Online] 28 November 2012. https://www.journalism.org/2012/11/28/role-social-media-arab-uprisings/.

43. **Finnemore and Sikkink.** *International norm dynamics and political change.* 1998.

44. **Lynch, Marc.** *Voices of the New Arab Public: Iraq, Al Jazeera and Middle East Politics today* . 2007.

45. **Momani, B.** *Arab Dawn: Arab youth and the demographic dividend they will bring.* 2015.

46. **Marzouk, Samah Gomaa Mohamed Abou.** NEGOTIATING THE INTERSECTION OF ARABIC AND ANGLOAMERICAN LITERARY JOURNALISM: EXPLORING POSSIBILITIES, CHALLENGING CANONS. 2017.

47. *Revisiting Putnam's two-level game theory in the digital age: domestic digital diplomacy and the Iran nuclear deal.* **Bjola, Corneliu and Manor, Ilan.** 2018, Cambridge Review of International Affairs, Vol. 31.

48. *Social Media Mobility: Leveraging Twitter Networks in Online Diplomacy.* **Manor, Ian and Segev, Elad.** 2020, Global Policy.

49. *Reassessing "Whose Story Wins":The Trajectory of Identity Resilience in Narrative Contests.* **Zaharna, R. S.** 2016, International Journal of Communication.

50. *Security branding and digital narrations. Security issues representation on Twitter.* **Anzera, Giuseppe, Gianturco, Giovanna and Massa, Alessandra.** 2019, INTERNATIONAL REVIEW OF SOCIOLOGY—REVUE INTERNATIONALE DE SOCIOLOGIE.

51. **O'reily .** [Online] https://www.oreilly.com/library/view/social-network-analysis/9781449311377/ch04.html.

52. **Twiplomacy study.** Twiplomacy study 2020. *Twiplomacy.com.* [Online] 2020. https://twiplomacy.com/blog/twiplomacy-study-2020/.

53. **Twiplomacy.** Twiplomacy WHO study. *Twiplomacy.com.* [Online] 2020. https://twiplomacy.com/blog/who-you-gonna-call/.

54. —. Twiplomacy study 2020. [Online] 2020. https://twiplomacy.com/blog/twiplomacy-study-2020/.

55. **Berelson, B.** *Content analysis in communication research.* 1952.

56. **Twiplomacy.** Twiplomacy study 2018. [Online] 2018. https://twiplomacy.com/blog/twiplomacy-study-2018/.

57. *Beyond the iconic protest images: the performance of 'everyday life' on social media during Gezi Park.* **McGarry, Aidan, et al.** 3, 2019, Social Movement Studies , Vol. 18.

Index

www.ingramcontent.com/pod-product-compliance
Lightning Source LLC
LaVergne TN
LVHW020414220926
848484LV00018B/2577/J
9781680532838